Fireflies *in a* Jar

A Milltown Reverie

GEORGIA NEJAK KRAFF

Fireflies in a Jar

Jason Kraff, Co-Creator
Cover design by Mina Widmer Design
Interior design by Jera Publishing

ISBN 978-0-9881788-0-9

Published by: Kaliad Publishing

Acknowledgments

I wish to thank my two wonderful sons, David and Jason, for their love and support and for never giving up on me.

David, thanks for always trying to keep my feet on the ground. Believe me, sometimes when I needed it most it worked. I am so proud that you are my son.

To Jason, thanks with all my heart for your editorial talents and penchant for fun and truth. You've helped me to create a legacy of my family for you, your brother Dave and my beautiful granddaughters, Kayla, Lily, Addison and Delaney. Most of the words written here reflect your input. A simple "thank you" is insufficient.

Thanks also to you both for humoring me by listening to these stories about my family so many times over the years and remembering things that I had forgotten. I love you guys beyond measure.

To my friend and original mentor, L.A. Justice for all the advice and encouragement given to a fledgling writer all those years ago.

To my superb editor Kevin Ramirez, and his lovely, patient and supportive wife Sasha – thank you for helping turn my dream into reality.

To my great friend and cheerleader, artist and poet Jane Hook Smith – thank you, thank you, for all the advice, laughs and invaluable input you gave to help me put just the right mood into the words on the page. Let's go have a pizza (with everything)!

To Christina Ranallo of PenPaperWrite – Your "Writers in the Dark" workshops were a true inspiration. The enthusiasm and creative energy you brought to every session were the catalysts that drove me to get these memories down on paper. From one Chicagoan to another...thanks buddy!

To the Thursday night writers' group – Ron Saint, Kim Muller, Michael McConnell, Mike Kennedy and Bill Gibson – your encouragement and honest critiques kept me on course. Many thanks!

And finally, to my family...Mom, Dad, George, Michael and Joey – without you there would be no story. I love and miss you all.

Reflections

If you had been sitting around a table in Chi-town drinking beer with my three brothers and me a couple of dozen years ago, these are the stories that you would have heard. We would have all been laughing and, as the night wore on, the stories would have taken on a life of their own. Whether reliving the catastrophe they barely escaped at the neighborhood tar pit or wondering how Michael hatched the scheme to earn money for carnival rides by swallowing goldfish, the revelry would have lasted long into the night. Never quite reaching the level of fabrication, those times would have nonetheless been remembered more and more through the gentle haze of nostalgia, along with the enhancement of more than a few pitchers of beer.

Although the names of neighbors and friends have been changed and some episodes consolidated to help with the flow of the tale, these stories of growing up on the East Side of Chicago in the 1950's are pretty much true. I sincerely hope that all those who shared in our lives will know that what is written here was written with love and respect. I also hope that their backbreaking contribution to the vibrancy that was once middle class America will be appreciated by all who read this.

The steel mills in my hometown are no more. The East Side has gone the way of so many other places in what was once the Industrial Heart of America, and is now known, sadly, as the Rust Belt.

It is my hope that in writing this story, the East Side as it once was will once again come to life for all who lived, worked and played there.

And to my brothers, George, Michael and Joey, I'd just like to say... I really, really miss you guys.

In the great scheme of things, none of us are here for long.

We are born, we grow, then we are gone.

As kids, we are lightning bugs. Bright spirits that seem to revel in just being alive.

We are oblivious to the waiting jars of those who would capture us.

Once caught, we are often forgotten and abandoned as our captors move on to their next adventure.

And the next.

If we are lucky, we will not be trapped and our lights will continue to glow and sparkle as long as we are here.

Sometimes, though, we offer ourselves.

We go willingly to the jar because that's where all the other bugs are now.

It's safe there, so we think.

We will be comfortable.

We won't have to worry about what tomorrow may bring.

Chapter 1

Home Again

THE DRIZZLE HARDENED into a driving rain as I ducked into the cab just off Wacker Drive and handed a piece of paper with the address of my destination to the driver. It had been eight years since I'd been back to my hometown. Truth be told, if not for an afternoon meeting downtown, I wouldn't be here today. The cab itself sent my mind in a spin. It was obvious that it had been through its share of Midwest summers and winters, judging from the rust around all the wheel wells and dents punctuating the doors and bumpers. Inside, the smell was of cheap perfume, stale cigarette smoke and the lingering, damp musk of floor mats infused with melted sleet and snow, even though it was closer to the next frost than the last.

"Whoa! Man… that *rain* sure got worse in a hurry!" the cabbie said in a familiar, flat Midwestern twang.

He glanced at me in the rearview mirror, then back at the street ahead. A moment later, his eyes shifted back to the mirror and his gaze lingered for a few seconds.

As he turned his attention back to the road, I gave his reflection in the mirror a long look, wondering…

Nah, I thought. *Never seen the guy before.*

"Coming home or just visiting?" he asked.

"Huh? Oh... visiting," I said softly, turning my gaze to the rain-spattered side window. Caught somewhere between past and present, I was overcome with emotion. Nostalgia swept over me, along with a feeling of profound sorrow and loss.

My thoughts were regularly interrupted by the seemingly clumsy navigation of the cab. Not the driver's fault, though. The streets were more riddled with potholes than I had remembered. There was a recent addition, at least as far as my last hometown recollection, of detour signs directing traffic around the abandoned railroad tracks and through a maze of haphazard street construction that kept cars driving in what seemed to be endless circles. All of this construction, yet not a single worker on site.

Man, I know Chicago's short on funds, but why the hell start something that you can't finish?

I placed the long box I had been holding in the passenger seat next to me, keeping my arm resting on it so that the precious contents wouldn't spill out onto the floor. Leaning back, I closed my eyes and let the memories return. The years melted away. I was back home.

The neighborhood where I grew up would never have been pictured on a postcard, nor would it have been the subject of a Currier and Ives print. When outsiders think of Chicago, they usually envision all the lights and drama of downtown, the magnificent mile of North Michigan Avenue or picturesque Lakeshore Drive. But to most native Chicagoans, it is the neighborhoods and their residents, more often than not from ethnic stock with rich and varied histories, that give Chi-town her swaggering charm. We lived quite a ways across town from Chicago's more desirable facets. The "East Side", whose name was derived from its location on the east bank of the Calumet River, was an eyesore. It was the kind of place that politicians always called the "Backbone of America." Every big city has these neighborhoods and we all know that politicians never seem to live among these "salt of the earth" people of whom they speak so highly.

Our neighborhood was bordered on one side by railroad tracks and suspension bridges. Commuter trains didn't run on the tracks, only freight trains bringing ore to the mill. The bridges over the Calumet River were often in the open position to allow for the passage of freighters that were also carrying raw materials to be used for steel production. The river ran from Lake Michigan right through town past the U.S. Steel South Works, Youngstown Steel, Wisconsin Steel, Acme/Interlake Steel and Republic Steel. Anyone trying to leave the East Side, whether for work or recreation, was often stopped cold by a freight train paused on the tracks or a raised bridge. There was no way around – we just had to wait until the train moved or the bridge lowered, then continue on our way. Natives called our hometown the "East Side Island" because of the difficulty we often encountered when venturing away from home. Some joked that we could just raise the bridges someday if we ever decided to secede from the city of Chicago.

The bungalow on Greenbay Avenue where I grew up was typical of the row upon row of nearly identical houses, shaded by elm trees. Often, the only way to differentiate one house from the next was to note which families didn't take their Christmas lights down 'til Easter or who still had a two-year-old rip in the front screen door. These were our neighborhood clues to the East Side's social pecking order. We were a proud, shabby bunch and no one liked to admit when they had fallen on hard times.

They were typical Midwestern homes, but my mother, being a pretentious romantic, called our house an East Coast Cape Cod. She had fallen in love with the song, "Old Cape Cod" by Patti Page and fancied herself living in New England, although she had never been any further east than Erie, Pennsylvania. Given the realities of life in our neighborhood, escapism was a favorite pastime.

Greenbay, an odd misnomer since there was no bay within 300 miles, green or otherwise, bordered a sticker-studded, snake-infested prairie that served as a buffer between the conglomeration of bungalows, taverns and churches that made up the residential area and the Republic Steel Mill that loomed beyond. At the far back edge of the prairie, just before the embankment that fronted the mill was a makeshift dump. Old car parts, mattresses, dead appliances and thousands of empty Richard's Wild Irish Rose wine and Schlitz beer bottles tossed out by the bums who rode the trains full of ore for the mill, lay waste there.

Next to the dump was a lagoon – which was really just a pit – filled to the brim with tar. Nobody knew how deep it was or how it got there. Like the moon and the stars, it was just there, an indisputable fact of nature, a small sea of black goo punctuated by twigs, dead bugs and a couple of hapless birds that had underestimated the stickiness of the mess. The prairie, dump, and tar pit, as it was known, were favorite recreational destinations for the neighborhood kids.

While the mill was in full swing, a constant gray haze hung in the South Chicago sky. The steel mills were responsible for much of the area's employment and nearly all of its smog.

Housewives hung laundry on backyard clotheslines, hoping for a few good hours of drying time before the mill let out its inevitable belch of pollution. They watched the skies like plane spotters during wartime, waiting for the first blast of smoke from the stacks. When it came, they ran to the lines, pulling off clothespins with lightning speed and hauling their family's socks, underwear and bed linens back into the safety of their sooty houses.

The fallout covered every snowfall with a reddish-black crust. The spring thaw left behind a layer of grime. The rains brought the higher-flying filth down, where the summer sun baked it onto rooftops and sidewalks. In warm weather, acrid heat rising from the pavement assaulted the sinuses and brought tears to the eyes.

It was only after moving away years later that I came to realize that the normal sky color on an average sunny day was a clear azure, so unlike the East Side skies that, on the brightest of days, were the hazy, grey-blue of a piece of beach glass, pummeled by waves and tossed to the shores of Lake Michigan.

Chapter 2

Freeze Tag, Fireflies, and Uncle Charlie the Ice Cream Man

MOST SUMMER EVENINGS in my old neighborhood began with a symphony. The sound of crickets and their nightly chirping blended melodically with the muffled rise and fall of the grown-ups' talk and laughter. Percussion was provided by ice tinkling in tall drink glasses and the sound of beer cans popping open. Once the relentless heat of the day had begun to wane, we could smell hot dogs and burgers on a myriad of grills, tended by the men… at least the ones who were home from the day shift at the mill.

I imagine similar scenes were playing out in thousands of other neighborhoods – the difference would be that in smaller towns, the activities might revolve more around church or a town square, complete with band shell. These romantic notions came to me from years of watching Rogers and Hammerstein musicals. I figured folks in those towns were a lot more wholesome and I wondered what they'd think if they knew about our parents' weeknight, backyard, alcohol-enhanced revelry and

Left:
Republic Steel Mill

Below:
Boys in tub

Below:
Georgia, Joey, George & Michael

time-honored weekend tradition of parking their rumps on barstools at the local tavern while the kids sat on the floor in sawdust, munching Slim Jims, mesmerized by the colors on the Wurlitzer jukebox.

But on ordinary weekday nights, when the after dinner drinks were poured and there was a danger of being drafted into cleanup duty, a throng of kids poured out of individual backyards and into the streets where there were games to be played and fireflies to be caught.

Freeze tag was an early lesson in cooperation. Theoretically, everybody stays in play until they are tagged by the "it" person. That freezes the tagged victim in place, who is allowed to neither speak, nor move a muscle until one of the other players unfreezes him. The non-speaking, non-movement law was strictly enforced by my younger brothers and their buds who spent much of their free time thinking up ever more outlandish punishments for transgressors. The last time I broke the rule, the rest of the gang gathered around me to watch with glee as I had to lick a big, green tomato worm, one of the most repulsive bugs on the planet.

Standing still on a summer night on the East Side of Chicago, however, could guarantee that the frozen victim would serve as a veritable buffet for mosquitoes. Maybe it was a combination of their exposure to the constant pollution fallout from Republic Steel and their steady diet of rich, ethnically-diverse East Side blood, but the mosquitoes in our neighborhood had somehow achieved a size and a viciousness one would expect from sub-tropical, prehistoric bugs.

Freeze tag would have been fun, except that since I was the only girl, I was considered a pariah – someone to be eliminated as quickly as possible. I wasn't the only outcast, however. Emil Jablonski, the puny, little, freckle-faced neighbor kid who was a constant target for the bigger boys' taunts, yet who idolized his tormentors (especially my brothers), was also a victim of quick and efficient elimination.

So Emil and I were always the first targets to be frozen. Our fellow players would even herd us toward the tagger, guaranteeing that we would be effectively out of the game. They could have just banned us from playing in the first place, but they knew that our folks wouldn't take kindly to such blatant discrimination. Once we were frozen, the two us would be immediately rendered invisible to all other players. We couldn't move or say anything, as that would incur one of the gang's unspeakable punishments. So there we would stand, Emil and I, like sweaty statues, each surrounded by a halo of enormous and ravenous mosquitoes. I wasn't disappointed at all when somebody yelled "Game's over!" and we all headed home to retrieve our Mason jars.

Back into the streets we'd go, jar lids punched with holes, grass on the bottom to keep the magical lights alive. It was just about the time that the fireflies had begun lighting up that we would hear a familiar ringing. Our neighborhood ice cream man, Uncle Charlie, usually made his rounds on the East Side just after dark. He pedaled a three-wheeled grownup tricycle with a freezer on the front. The reason he came after dark was so he could avoid dealing with us. Uncle Charlie hated kids. Or maybe he just hated us. I think he spent his prime selling time unloading his goods a few streets over where the kids had more money. (It seemed that the further away from the mill you lived, the higher your social status.)

We would run up to his trike, grubby hands clutching nickels and dimes and ask, "Whatcha got?"

His ice cream would always be half-melted and the Popsicles so stale that the syrup stuck to the soggy wrapper, but Uncle Charlie acted like he was selling caviar to swine.

"Jeeeeezzz! Youse kids are a pain in my ass," he'd whine. "Can't ya's ever figure out what ya's want before youse come clammerin' aroun'?!"

Undeterred, we'd gape at the faded pictures on the side of his cart of ice cream sandwiches, chocolate and nut-topped cones and Push-ups. Invariably, the stuff we wanted was always gone and we'd have to settle for whatever Uncle Charlie actually had in his freezer. Which wasn't much. After all, the kids from the "better" side of town had already had their pick of the litter an hour ago. The stuff we bought was only in the cart to keep the previously sold frozen treats cold. We were essentially buying his packing material.

Clutching our melting Popsicles, with syrup running down our arms and attracting flies from a three-state radius, we began our quest to capture the blinking golden lights.

Once, a cousin told me that if I pulled off the tail of a lightning bug, the glow would stay and I could wear it on my finger like a ring.

So I did.

My cousin was right! The small golden jewel glowed on my finger. As I admired it, I glimpsed the defrocked firefly crawling painfully away before dying. Then I looked down at my firefly ring, and the glowing jewel had become just a glob of pale yellow goo.

I ran over to the porch where all our captured fireflies glittered in Mason jars. Though only in captivity a short while, they already looked sluggish. Unscrewing the lids, I watched the bugs rise into the night, blinking and dancing against the background of elm trees and bungalows.

In the dark distance, the sky above the Republic Steel Mill glowed orange and angry, as the night shift laborers toiled at their trades and dreamed of the day they could carry their lunch pails home for the last time.

Chapter 3

Popsicle Sticks and Comic Books

THOUGH THE EAST SIDE was nobody's idea of paradise, most people kept their grass trimmed, shutters painted and fences in decent repair. Most, that is, except for the Crump clan.

Nobody remembers exactly when the unholy brood descended on our neighborhood. The folks who vacated the house never bothered to say goodbye. They must've realized what a blight they were bequeathing their former neighbors and wanted to "get outta Dodge" before the crap hit the fan.

Later on, it was difficult for us to recall how the once tidy bungalow transitioned into the ramshackle hovel it became. The change seemed sudden and catastrophic – like the devastation a tsunami might wreak after a picture-perfect day at the beach.

My first encounter with a Crump came on a sunny Saturday afternoon in Mid-June.

"Go down to Harry and Mary's and get a loaf of bread," my mom said. "An' make sure there's no hole in the wrapper!" I thought back on the last loaf I had brought home that had been rendered inedible to all but the scrawny sparrows in our backyard because of a small tear in the seal. I promised to be more careful this time.

I didn't mind going to the store for my mother since I always got a little extra change for some candy – and in the early '50's, you could get quite a stash for five cents. Penny candy cost a cent, and sometimes you could get a "two-fer," but the two-fers weren't the best. I wanted to make sure my investment was a wise one. No doubt the dentist, whose office was above Harry and Mary's grocery, also had a vested interest in their candy selection. Half his business came from the fillings pulled out by Mary Janes and cracked molar jawbreaker casualties.

Strolling along, oblivious to the menace that awaited me, I started to sing to myself.

"Ohhhhhh the buzzin' of the bees in the cinnamon trees and the soda waaaaaater fountain, the lemonade springs and the bluebird sings in the Big Rock Caaaaaaaaandy Mountai–"

From the corner of my eye, I spied a sudden movement. Cackling maniacally, a boy jumped out of the bushes, brandishing a sharp thing.

A KNIFE?! I was horrified. But it wasn't a knife.

It was a Popsicle stick, honed to a sharp point and it looked lethal.

"Yew got money?" he screeched, waving his weapon in my face.

Since most East Siders spoke with a distinct Midwestern twang, his snarl through that unfamiliar hillbilly accent made what he said even more sinister.

"N-n-n-n-no," I stammered. "I mean, yeah. I got money... but I gotta buy bread... for my ma."

"Gimme dat money!" His teeth were brown and crooked and his choppy haircut and scalp full of cowlicks made his flat head look like a cow pie. "Ah am Billy Joe Crump an' Ah'm th' bawss 'roun heah!"

Above:
House on Greenbay

Left:
Neighborhood Kids

I forked over the bread and candy money. He snatched it, then poked me in the arm with the stick. Hard.

"Owwww! What's THAT for? I GAVE YOU MY MONEY!" I howled.

"Thass so's yew remembuh who's thuh bawss!" he sneered. Running, he yelled back over his shoulder, "An' eff yew tayell ennybuddy Ah took yer dough, AH'LL GIT YEW!"

I turned around and headed home to face my mother, miserable at the prospect.

"WHAT?" she hollered, her neck blossoming with crimson blotches. "Summbitch! Them damn hillbillies! Which one of them kids took that money?"

She then let loose a stream of profanity in both English and Polish. I thought for a fleeting second that maybe I had a partner in arms, someone to have my back and right this terrible wrong. It was, after all, my candy money that had been lost. When I didn't reply, she mumbled, "Ah, never mind. I don't know how the hell you'd know which one it was. Them Crumps got about 15 kids and they all look alike. Beady eyes, rotten teeth and pork pie heads." She seemed to be leaving it at that for the time being and I was actually relieved since Billy Joe's parting words that he was gonna git me still rang in my ears.

There weren't actually 15 kids in the Crump family and they didn't all look alike. Some were even kind of cute, in an offbeat way. Little Darcy Lou, the baby, would sometimes amble down the block, her loaded diaper drooping, as she bribed the neighborhood dogs and cats with a cookie. When they came close, she hugged them, kissed their heads and toddled off, picking her nose and grinning. Darcy Lou was the only toddler I've ever seen who wore lace-up boots, the kind that my brothers called "shit kickers." She was learning the family trade early on.

For the first few months the Crumps lived in the middle of our block, the other neighborhood kids stayed close to home. The immediate neighbors on either side of their shack had reported that they'd seen the family patriarch, Big Joe Crump, firing a shotgun into the prairie that backed up to our street. Nobody knows what he was shooting at, but we all figured it might be dinner, since no one had ever seen old lady Crump in the grocery store, or anyplace else outside of the trash-festooned dirt heap that served as their front yard.

There was also a local legend that Big Joe once shot a railroad bum and the family cooked him up and ate him for dinner. It was rumored that Big Joe threw the bones into the tar pit, but kept the guy's clothes to wear. My brothers and their buddies whispered that if you looked real close you could see the holes from the buckshot in his red flannel shirt. I never questioned this, even though no one outside of the Crump family had ever gotten close enough to the old man to verify.

The cumulative I.Q. of the entire brood probably didn't hit double digits, but what Billy Joe lacked in intelligence, he more than made up for in sneaky shrewdness and an uncanny ability to know when I was out in the neighborhood.

Billy and the rest of the Crump kids were social outcasts, but everybody in the neighborhood knew that my brothers and I had an extensive comic book collection. If I had no money when Billy Joe hit me up, he'd demand that I go back home, gather up several comic books and fork them over. "If you squeal, I'm gonna git ya," he'd hiss.

For a while, I managed to cover my tracks by picking out ones that I figured wouldn't be missed by my brothers. But after a couple of weeks, Billy Joe was no longer satisfied with Little Lulu and Nancy and Sluggo. He demanded Superman.

"How about Popeye?" I offered.

"Superman!" Billy yelled.

But as so often happens in life, greed ended Billy's gravy train. George and Michael, noticing that a few of the issues starring their favorite superhero had gone missing, caught me trying to sneak out of the house with a couple of their most valued comics. As I scooted out the screen door, my brothers, stone-faced with arms-crossed, blocked my path.

"Waaaaaaa! Billy Joe... comic books... candy money... GIT ME!" I blubbered.

That was enough to send the two older Nejak boys, accompanied by their sniveling sister, down the block where we found Billy Joe squatting on the sidewalk, sharpening another lethal Popsicle stick. Sensing danger, he glanced up from his task. Beady eyes narrowing and nostrils flaring, his cocky grin wavered. Billy stood, but rather than attacking, he began to back away. Then he suddenly turned and made a run for it.

Michael stood in the middle of the sidewalk blocking his escape route. When the dust settled, Billy Joe ended up with two black eyes and a bloody nose. It may have been vigilante justice, but it worked.

Years later, I heard that Billy Joe had become a resident of the Illinois State Prison at Joliet. Apparently his weapon of choice was more deadly than a Popsicle stick. There would be no mill job, at least in the near future, for Billy. Rather than spend days and nights on end working among blast furnaces and piles of coal like the rest of the men, he whiled away his time surrounded by gray cinderblock walls and barred doors and windows.

He did manage, in a way, to escape his dismal situation by developing his artistic side. Ironically, Billy's prior dexterity with transforming Popsicle sticks into murder weapons came in handy there. Rumor has it that he was held in high esteem by the other inmates for the perfectly detailed miniature giraffes, sailboats and toy soldiers he fashioned out of scrap wood. Billy Joe, former junior outlaw, had finally found something that he excelled at. He turned out to be a model prisoner.

Chapter 4

A Fish Tale

EVERY SUMMER, OUR local Catholic church hosted a carnival that transformed the dirt and weed-covered schoolyard into a bizarre landscape of wildly spinning, crashing and gyrating torture devices, loosely referred to as "rides." Beer, soda and gut-busting food concession stands formed an aisle that ended in a row of tents housing games of chance that neatly skirted the Chicago gambling laws. One such tent sheltered a Bingo set-up, which, only two days into the carnival season, was shut down by the local police for being in violation of a recently proclaimed law against Bingo. It's not that Chicago was such a city of holy-rollers as much as knowing whose palms to grease.

Apparently, somebody knew who and how because the next day all the Bingo cards had been reprinted with the word "LUCKY." Rather than "B-5" being hollered over the loud speaker, it was now "L-5!" It took a while for the locals to catch on to the new system though, and some poor schmuck would invariably yell, "BING… ey" rather than LUCKY.

During the early years of its run, our parish carnival was the scene of a mini-scandal when the church pastor won the car raffle two years in a row. Sister Superior, who drew the winning ticket both years declared it a "miracle." But when the bishop got wind of it, he proclaimed that two such unbelievable occurrences in two consecutive years involving both the priest and a new Dodge was, in his esteemed opinion, one miracle too many. He declared a moratorium on miracles, unless statues began to weep blood or it started raining ten dollar bills.

The church carnival was heaven on earth for the East Side kids. My three brothers were the ultimate ride junkies – the sicker they got, the better they liked it. One memorable year, middle brother, Michael, having blown his entire allowance in the first 20 minutes of opening day, set up shop next to the Win a Goldfish tent. The older kids were crazy about this game where they had to toss Ping Pong balls into small bowls, each housing a live fish. A true test of skill in the minds of the teenage boys was to win a goldfish for their girlfriends. They really didn't care about the fish. The poor things would usually die within a week and be flushed down the john.

Michael decided it would be a wise business decision to charge the winners a quarter apiece to watch him swallow their new pet. It saved them the trouble of carrying a plastic water-filled bag around all night, not to mention the cost of food and care. The benefit to Michael, of course, was that each quarter would buy him another ride on something that rotated, jerked and lurched. He told me years later that it wasn't such a bad gig. Gulping down the fish was easy, he explained, and relatively quick and painless (except maybe for the fish). As long as Michael kept his mind focused

Uncle Ralph, Aunt Diane, Dad and Mom

on the fun he'd have later, everything was dandy. The only unpleasant incidents were the couple of times when one of the fish made a last-ditch effort to "swim back upstream."

It wasn't long before Michael, hands in pockets jingling his newfound wealth, set out in search of the two others to join him in experiencing the thrills of the midway. The three ran smack into our mother, our aunt Diane and me as we emerged from the gaming tent, each of them clutching a beer and me munching on a corn dog. Aunt Diane, our dad's younger sister, was always up for a good time. Our mother held up her latest prize – a grinning, black, plastic cat clock with shifting eyes, a pendulum tail and two rotating hands in the middle of its stomach.

"Hey you boys, how d'ya think this'll look on the wall above the Frigidaire?" our mother asked, while our aunt handed me her beer and waved her new 8 millimeter movie camera at her nephews, hollering, "Get on a ride boys. I'll make Hollywood stars out of ya's!"

George, Michael, and Joey turned and waved at Aunt Diane's camera lens as they prepared to board The Scrambler – a torturous device with two long metal arms with buckets on the end. Basically, a giant Mixmaster with seats where the beaters would have been, it was just the right size for three young boys, including one with a bellyful of recently-consumed goldfish.

The ride started slowly at first and our aunt with her camera were positioned so that each time the bucket containing my brothers came around, it headed straight toward her before spinning out of range. Michael's expression morphed from an enormous grin to a forced smirk, and finally, into something resembling a green death mask. In the last few frames, as their car once again headed toward the camera, his lolling head had dropped onto the safety bar.

After what seemed like hours on the carnival ride-from-hell, the ride operator – who had been entranced in a conversation with a pretty teenage girl – finally remembered to wind the monster down. My three brothers staggered off. George and

Joey wore tepid smiles. Michael lurched toward our aunt, eyes rolling, mouth agape and up came a stream of half-digested hot dogs, funnel cakes, taffy apples and goldfish – all of it landing on her shiny black shoes.

Not wanting to let a great film-worthy situation go to waste, she panned from Michael to the gathering crowd, then to our panic-stricken mother, rushing to the aid of her sick son.

The incredible episode ended with the camera lens coming to rest on the ground, where the now forgotten cat clock lay grinning maniacally.

Michael returned to the carnival year after year, not only enhancing his original act by swallowing two at once, but also adding juggling and sleight-of-hand tricks. Over time, he built quite a sizeable local following.

My other brothers became Michael's shills without even getting a piece of the action. It could have been the sheer glory of being in "showbiz" or maybe it was the simple amazement they felt in watching their sibling ingest live aquatic life forms. To them, Michael wasn't just a neighborhood oddity. His talents brought a claim to fame for our whole family, however dubious it might be.

As our parents garnered pieces of these shenanigans from our neighbors and added them to tidbits of whispered secrets caught in snatches of conversations between my brothers, they began to look at middle son Michael with awe and concern. Entrepreneurship was not a trait ordinarily nurtured in most East Side families. The expectation was that the offspring of mill workers would eventually become mill workers themselves. If somebody's kid went to college and became a doctor or dentist, that kid would become an East Side doctor or dentist and work on the bodies and teeth of mill workers and their families.

But what about a kid who swallowed goldfish and juggled oranges? Ringling Brothers Circus never came to the East Side and if it did, could their son make a living doing what he seemed to do best: unconventional, yet entertaining things?

"What would become of Michael?" they wondered.

Chapter 5

A Fourth of July Barbeque and Johnny Spankovic's Barge

THE FOURTH OF JULY dawned hot and hazy. Our Indiana relatives were coming over for the annual Nejak Lamb Roast and Fireworks Extravaganza. It was also the long-awaited day that our neighbor would launch his salvage business on the barge that he had been constructing for the past year. Later on, the Spankovics, our family and a host of admiring relatives and neighbors would follow the flatbed truck that carried Johnny Spankovic's creation to the Calumet River for its maiden voyage.

Our kitchen was a frenzy of activity. The grey Formica table was laden with hard-boiled eggs, chopped onions and celery, fresh parsley and Hellman's mayonnaise (the *only* kind of mayonnaise there was, according to our mother). The radio set on the counter blared out the Sox game. They were in town and to our dad, all was right with the world.

As mom concocted an enormous potato salad, the old man labored over his masterpiece – a leg of lamb that he lovingly rubbed with smashed garlic and his special spice recipe, which was a sophisticated blend of salt, pepper, and some obscure green herb.

He massaged the lamb, kneading the garlic and seasoning mixture into fat and flesh like a master masseuse. He either didn't know or didn't care that George and Michael were in the basement, rummaging through his recently purchased arsenal of fireworks in delirious anticipation of the evening's pyrotechnics.

Meanwhile, six-year-old brother Joey was in the backyard teaching his new pet, Blackie the Wonder Dog, a trick he was sure would dazzle our relatives. The pooch was learning to scale our only tree in order to fetch an empty beer can. Joe climbed up to a crook in the branches, wedged the can into the notch, and dropped to the ground yelling, "Fetch Blackie! Good dog! Wanna beer? Ha-ha-ha-ha-ha."

The dog backed up, ran full bore at the tree, leapt and wrapped his front legs around the trunk. He then nudged himself upwards with his back claws, all the while keeping his eyes on the prize, a squashed Pabst Blue Ribbon can. His concentration was unshakeable.

A month earlier, Joey had arrived home with Blackie, a stray with no collar or tags, trailing behind. The mutt looked as though he'd been riding the box cars with the Hobos. He was spunky though, with loads of personality and Joey was sure he could be spiffed up with a bath and his unruly, spiked, ebony fur combed neatly or perhaps tamed with a little Brylcreem. But no matter what Joey tried to improve his appearance, Blackie continued to look like he'd been groomed by a pack of rabid wolverines.

Nevertheless, the dog was proving himself enormously talented. Unfortunately, he was also oversexed. For the next several years until Blackie suddenly disappeared (we assumed to join a traveling dog show), he sired dozens of mini-Blackies. At that time, having a pet fixed or snipped was not high priority since money was always tight. Consequently, most of our neighbors had canine or feline extended families with the rest of the East Side.

Blackie's favorite girlfriend was Queenie, a neighbor's dachshund-collie mix. Try as they might to keep their pet away from the amorous Blackie, he proved himself too clever for them. In one case, Queenie's owner called our mother and described the scene that was playing out in her backyard as she spoke. Blackie was makin' whoopee with hot-to-trot Queenie *through* their chain link fence.

But I digress. It was the Fourth of July, the morning haze had burned off, and the sun seemed to pulse with heat. Our father, having prepped his culinary *piece de resistance* and reverently placed it in the fridge to cool before cooking, was scooping a layer of grime and bugs off the top of the water in our new above-ground pool. I use the term "pool" loosely, as it was more of a large metal cake dish that was fourteen inches deep and twelve feet in diameter. After skimming the pool, he tossed in three enormous inner tubes which took up much of the available "swimming" space.

George and Michael, having temporarily forgotten about the explosives in the basement, were enthralled, watching our neighbor, Johnny Spankovic, put the finishing touches on the barge he had been constructing for the past year in the prairie behind the two flat that housed the Spankovic family. Month after month, the boys and their friends thrilled at the sight of an enormous vessel being created from empty oil drums and scrap metal. They would watch late into the evening, the sparks of the welding arc hypnotizing them into dreams of someday creating their own barges. Or stock cars. Or rocket ships.

Johnny worked at the mill as a talented welder, but his dream was to be a boat captain - specifically to be captain of a salvage barge, built with his own two hands. He would pilot down the river, dredging for junk. Prior to embarking on his barge construction, Johnny worked on jalopies that he raced at the local stock car track. His pioneering spirit had already established him as somewhat of a celebrity with the neighborhood kids and parents alike.

Finally, the day had arrived. The plan was that after the cheering throngs had watched the launch of our neighbor's new business venture at the canal, we'd all head back to Greenbay Avenue to eat, drink and be merry. The festivities would climax with a dazzling fireworks display put on by the old man and his pyromaniac buddies, celebrating the births of both our nation and the Spankovic Salvage Company, Inc.

At 2:30, assorted aunts, uncles and cousins began showing up. Bowls of bean salad, Jell-O molds and trays of brownies joined our mother's potato salad and the old man's lamb in the refrigerator. The men opened beers and joined my brothers in the backyard in anticipation of the arrival of the flatbed truck that would transport Johnny's barge to its destination. Johnny extinguished his welding torch, flipped up his hood and waved to the admiring crowd. The men and boys waved back, awe-struck at the thought that a master craftsman was in their midst.

Hearing the sound of large, heavy tires on gravel, we turned to see the flatbed backing toward Johnny's barge. A ramp was lowered and a heavy chain was attached the front of the craft. Within minutes, Johnny's masterpiece had been pulled onto the truck bed. The boat was way too big to fit comfortably as it spilled over on three sides. Its craftsmanship was already being tested. It could very well have cracked in half under the pressure of its own weight. Our family, along with several dozen neighbors, headed for the street to begin the parade to the mighty Calumet.

Some drove through the East Side, but all of us kids followed on our bikes. The truck bearing Johnny's magnificent creation lead the way, red flags tied to the back flapping in the wind. It was some three miles to the river, much further than most kids ever rode on their bikes. The excitement of the day made it worth the trip. Most of us had never been included in the few parades that we had in our neighborhood. Being a part of this was, to us, equivalent to being a part of the Rose Bowl Parade. We felt like big cheeses. The select few. Friends of Johnny Spankovic.

When we arrived at the river, the neighbors left their cars and we kids dropped our bikes. We all gathered to watch as the flatbed backed to the edge of the seawall and lowered its scraped and dinged metal ramp to allow the vessel to slide onto the water. Small, murky waves lapped at the mossy, rust-encrusted wall. As we knew what heroic effort had gone into its creation, the river seemed unworthy of such a mighty craft.

An enormous cheer went up as the barge headed down the ramp. The tip of the craft was now touching the waves. Then... it was in!

Applause, handshakes and hugs all around. Everyone was so overjoyed and congratulatory that nobody noticed for a few minutes that the boat had disappeared.

"No! Oh no! Oh... my barge!" yelled Johnny.

Rushing to the edge of the seawall, we watched as twelve months of labor and a lifetime of dreams sank to the bottom of the waterway, ironically becoming the largest piece of salvage ever to crash into its muddy bottom.

Heading home, the mood had changed from celebratory to funereal. We all felt bad for Johnny and his family, but somehow his lost dream had personally touched each of us, young and old alike. Our neighborhood didn't produce movie stars or famous artists, but the thought of a mill worker, one of our own, having an ambitious wish come true meant there was hope for one and all.

Back on Greenbay, we disembarked the cars, left our bikes, and everyone except the Spankovics headed for our backyard, the planned site of the after-launch picnic. Grownups spoke in hushed tones, too crushed to be jovial. The ladies discussed whether to take some plates of food over to Johnny's family to get them through this sad time.

Then an amazing thing happened. The Spankovics came through our gate, Mrs. Spankovic carrying loaves of fresh baked bread, their kids carrying baskets of tomatoes and cucumbers from their garden, and Johnny carrying a glass of what looked like a quadruple shot of something brown. He forced a small smile, shook his head, took a swig from his glass, then broke into a wide grin. He joined the other men, clapped a few on the back, looked over to where his barge had stood until its fateful trip, and immediately launched into his plan to start another barge project in the morning. "Hell. Somebody's gotta get that old heap off the bottom of the Calumet!" he boomed.

The charcoal was smoldering in the grill with the lamb turning above, bits of grease hitting the coals with a garlicky hiss. A few guys gathered around the old man, drinks in hand, intensely watching the meat rotate as if they expected it to do something other than cook. Occasionally, our dad would test the meat's progress by gingerly shaving off a small piece and tossing it, still sizzling, into his mouth, oblivious to his scorched and blistering fingers.

"Mmmmmm... boy, dat's gooood!" I think it needs some more of my special spice though!" An' I think I need another drink!"

By mid-afternoon, picnic tables were laden with the home-made best of our family and neighbors. As the ladies removed waxed paper from the top of the dishes, Republic Steel let out an enormous belch, filling the skies with orange smoke. All eyes shifted upward, then down to where red dust settled onto our supper.

"Damn mill," our mother mumbled, looking forlornly down at what appeared to be an overly generous sprinkling of paprika on her potato salad.

Later, as evening fell, our father headed to the basement to retrieve his prized stash of fireworks. Boxes of sparklers were doled out to the kids, but George and Michael weren't a part of the grasping throng. Earlier, they had filled their pockets with lady fingers and cherry bombs. Our dad didn't seem to miss these, as his mind was now wrapped around the impressive figure he would be, arm extended, clutching his favorite, the Roman candle. He loved the hiss, then the firing of the vibrantly colored fireballs – *poonk, poonk, poonk* – from the end of the tube. The old man chortled in anticipation.

The multi-colored fountains were a favorite of the ladies. I ran with the other sparkler holders to any adult with a pack of matches. Soon the pungent smell of spent gunpowder filled the air, mingling with the enraptured *ooohs* and *ahhhs* of the ladies enjoying the rainbow-hued showers of sparks swirling around what the old man called "sissy fireworks."

George and Michael, of course, had their own matches, but couldn't admit this, as their explosives, as well as the matches, would have been immediately confiscated. So they headed across the alley to the prairie for the privacy that their underage revelry required.

It wouldn't be long before wails were heard, as the second a sparkler went out, its holder would immediately drop it on the spot and run to have another lit. As we were all barefoot, and since sparklers were basically metal rods that held their heat forever after the spark show was over, it was a rare kid who didn't go to bed that night with several long burn marks on foot bottoms.

Once the display was done and the grownups were having their nightcap of highballs or rum and cokes and a last cigarette before heading home, our gang took the opportunity to grab our jars and catch a few lightning bugs.

That night, lying in my room under the eaves, I heard thunder, then the comforting sound of a mid-summer shower on the roof close above my head. It had been a perfect day, I thought, in spite of the unfortunate barge incident.

The next morning as the sun rose, I sat on our front stoop and surveyed the soggy, charred cardboard cones and dead sparklers that would need to be cleaned up. A fine mist of gritty red dust from the mill was already beginning to pepper the sidewalk. Something glinted in the grass. A glass jar. I went over to where it lay on its side and picked it up. Inside, floating in a miniature lake of rainwater were a few twigs, a dandelion and three dead fireflies.

Chapter 6

In The Pits

AN AERIAL VIEW of our neighborhood from June 1st through the end of August would have looked like an ant farm populated by tiny sunburned maniacs engaged in a deliriously wild frenzy of activities – many of them capable of causing death or a similarly awful fate.

It didn't matter whether the sun blazed relentlessly, as it often did over the Southside prairies, or the rains fell in big, plump summer drops that hit the ground and burst like overripe berries, we were outside from dawn 'til whenever the grown-ups noticed the house was unusually quiet and tracked us down. By the time we were dragged home, any inch of us not covered by Band Aids over the results of prior calamities was sporting several mosquito bites the size of golf balls.

The year that my brothers decided to conquer the tar pit and reluctantly allowed their biggest fan, puny little Emil Jablonsky, into their scheme was a time that, for our family, would live in infamy. It also prompted the kid's mom to declare the Nejak boys off limits to her son. Forever. Or at least until she managed to scrub the last blotch of tar off of his hide. Little brother Joe was still too young to be a part of their adventures – and besides, our mother kept a wary eye on him. She knew what an irresistible pull George and Michael had on a smaller kid's psyche and she was annoyed that Joey, who was a handful himself, was always left behind in her charge.

But Mrs. Jablonsky had no such reservations about her son. She had told our mother that she knew how much Emil looked up to my brothers. She had no idea why, but she considered Emil a terrific judge of character. If they were ok with Emil, well then, by God, they were ok with her. Besides, Emil was a pest. And so letting him go off on a quest with the Nejak boys rather than hanging around the house under her feet couldn't be bad. Could it?

The arrival of a new appliance in any neighborhood household was always a major event for the family's kids. We didn't care that whatever the device did would conceivably make life easier for the adults. So what? They had nothing but time on their hands.

It wasn't the appliance itself that set our minds spinning. No -- a new appliance always came packaged in a large cardboard box that spelled only one thing. Recreation. Forts, sleds, imaginary space ships, the possibilities were endless. And the year of the tar pit incident was a veritable cardboard bonanza.

When the Sears delivery truck pulled up in front of our bungalow, my brothers' eager, grubby faces were plastered up against the front room window watching as *three* enormous appliance cartons were unloaded and dollied through our screen door. They waited impatiently as the washer, dryer, and water heater were unpacked and put into place.

"Uhhhh, can we have the boxes now?" George ventured, as Michael feigned non-interest.

"Go ahead... just be careful" our mother warned. "The last time you kids got ahold of one of these boxes, you almost broke your necks sledding down the basement stairs."

"Line up men! We're heading down to the pit!" George ordered, the self-appointed group leader. Michael fell in line right behind his older sibling, with little Emil, gap-toothed and grinning, bringing up the rear. As I watched them start their pit-bound trek, I left our backyard and followed. I was far enough behind, and they were so preoccupied that I was, at least for the time being, unnoticed. Though I was hardly ever allowed into their schemes, this I had to see.

Blond crew cuts shone in the sun as three young boys made their way down the alley that led from Greenbay Avenue through the prairie that fronted the mill to the tar pit. Six skinny legs stuck out of swim trunks and ended in cowboy boots. Emil sported a coonskin cap, a nod to his idol Davey Crockett. Each adventurer carried a cardboard box. Nobody spoke. They were Men on a Mission. As they made their way down the alley, the sun-scorched prairie on either side hummed with midsummer sounds.

Finally it lay before them. The smelly sludge seemed to undulate in the sweltering heat. Each boy tossed his flattened box onto the black mess.

Then, bending his knees to work up momentum, George sprang onto the closest box. Wavering slightly as the tar shifted below, he gingerly made his way to the edge of the cardboard to jump over to box number two.

Suddenly, anxious to impress his older friends with his fearlessness, and with total disregard of age etiquette, Emil Jablonsky leapt past Michael and landed squarely in the middle of box number one, still occupied by the now startled George. Immediately, two things happened. The cardboard collapsed in the middle, sinking Emil knee deep in tar, while catapulting George over the side and back onto the alley.

Emil's triumphant grin quickly gave way to a look of horror as he sank to his hips, then to his waist. He was going down like a rock. As Emil wildly flailed his arms and screeched, my mind raced back to the last Davey Crockett TV episode I had seen, in which a hapless trapper stumbled into a pool of quicksand. The scene that had made the biggest impression on my brain was the final shot of the quicksand, where the unfortunate man's hat rested atop the pool, surrounded by diminishing bubbles, ostensibly being produced by the now sunken trapper. When the kid's ear-piercing wails rose another two octaves – *Hellllllllp!* – I sprang into action. Covering my eyes and starting to cry, I turned to run home and hide under my bed until whatever happened, happened. But I froze in my tracks. I couldn't run away from the unfolding catastrophe – I had to help if I could.

Frantically turning to the adjacent dump in search of a rescue aid, George spied an old broom. He grabbed it, handed it to me and I thrust the bristled end toward the still sinking and now helplessly whimpering Emil. The kid grabbed for the broom and missed. Stretching as far as his skinny arms could reach, he grabbed again. Missed.

With rivulets of tears streaming down his grimy face, Emil, nearly exhausted, squeezed his eyes shut and stretched one last time. This time, he grasped the straw end. I began to pull with my two brothers behind me, adrenaline pumping, pulling with all their eight and ten-year-old strength. Miraculously, with an enormous sucking sound, Emil was dredged from the goop, his cowboy boots and swim trunks forever mired back in the tar. His entire ensemble now consisted of socks that dangled half off his feet and his naked body, covered with the sticky mess.

Apparently not appreciating the fact that his buddies and their sister had rescued him from a really close call, the little ingrate's wail rose to a fever pitch as he ran down the alley toward home.

"Maaaaaaaa... look what they made me doooooooooo!"

As he ran, tears and snot running down his cheeks, Emil's tar-covered feet picked up gravel. By the time he arrived at the Jablonsky back porch, I imagined that his feet, looking for all the world like gigantic, nut-covered taffy apples, weighed fifteen pounds apiece.

Before heading home, I hid my relief, shot a menacing look at my two heroic younger brothers and hissed, "If you guys tell Ma that I was anywhere near here when this happened, you're goners."

I proceeded to mentally rationalize my self-distancing from the situation at hand by figuring that there must have been many times that our parents imposed a blanket punishment on the four of us when I played no role in the escapade that prompted said punishment. The fact that it also went the other way and that my brothers also had shared the blame for some bone-headed stunt that I alone had pulled had no bearing on the current situation, I figured. So there.

Emil was grounded for a month. And when Mrs. Jablonsky spilled the beans to our mother about my brothers' adventure, she blurted out one of her classic, over-the-top punishments.

"You guys are grounded! For ten years!"

George and Michael cast baleful looks my way. I smiled sympathetically, shrugged my shoulders and sat down at our kitchen table with a comic book and a glass of chocolate milk.

On day one of their sentence, my brothers, as they plucked dandelions out of the front lawn, grudgingly helping the old man in his relentless battle against renegade weeds, took to incessant griping about how they had been set up by Emil. They didn't know what he could've been thinking, they said, when he suggested heading down to the tar pit with those boxes. They *knew,* after all, that the place was off limits. But Emil, they observed to our mother, didn't care about rules like that.

On day number two, as they each manned a push broom to sweep down the front steps and sidewalk, my brothers tried another angle. Emil would've become just another tar-pit casualty along with the poor birds and frogs that had been forever swallowed up by the pit, they insisted, had it not been for their heroic efforts. It was this last tactic, they were sure, that would begin to soften our mother's resolve. Not a chance.

The third day began with our father greeting them at the breakfast table with scrub brushes and a bucket of soapy water.

"I think it's about time the basement floor got a good scrubbing," he grumbled. "That damn dog's made a real mess down there."

Although Blackie was a marvelously gifted dog in some ways, he could never get over thinking that the world was his private latrine.

A couple of hours later, my brothers emerged from the basement smelly, sweaty and miserable.

"Go play out back till supper," our mother instructed. "But don't you dare leave the yard – you guys are still grounded. Just keep yourselves busy!"

I sat at the kitchen table, watching as our mother mixed together beef, pork and rice for our dinner of stuffed cabbage. She always put one stuffed pepper in the middle of the pot for the old man. It was a small concession that she made to his role as head of the household. While blending the meat, she began to add the seasonings. A shake of pepper, then mix. A shake of salt, and mix a little more. Then, as she glanced up at our kitchen window, I watched my mother's eyes take on a faraway look, a look that was coming frequently to her these days. Although the view outside the window was dominated by the Republic Steel Mill, she seemed to be focused on something else. On the kitchen table lay a magazine clipping that, from my perspective, looked to be of a couple sipping drinks under a large umbrella. The view in the background was of mountains and a stream. She had been clipping pictures like this for a while now. Sometimes they were of mountains, sometimes of lakes. But all featured happy people (no kids in sight) enjoying life in idyllic settings. I figured that maybe she was planning our next vacation.

"Mom?" I said, when I noticed that she was now pouring salt in a steady stream into the meat. "Hey, mom?"

Startled, she looked at me, then down at the mixing bowl. She put the salt container down and grabbed a spoon to remove the mound of salt that now covered the meat.

Later, after pouring tomato sauce into the pot with the stuffed cabbages and green pepper, our mother glanced out the window to the backyard. George and Michael each carried an armload of wood to add to a pile they had made in the far back corner.

"Well, at least they're keeping themselves busy... maybe this mess finally taught 'em a lesson," she said. "Wait! Where did that wood come from? There are no logs back there!"

She looked out the window for a moment, then gasped, "OH NO!" With her hands full of ground meat, she lurched toward the back door. There, on the cement patio, next to the place where our mother's new redwood patio set had formerly stood, was George's last birthday gift – a Handy Andy Tool Kit. It came complete with miniscule tools which, in the last couple of hours, had gotten their first (and last) real workout.

"What the HELL... are you guys NUTS?!" she sputtered. George and Michael turned, one holding the saw, the other a hammer and wrench, with looks of complete bewilderment. Hadn't she said that they should keep themselves busy, after all? What was the big deal?

"You put my furniture back the way it WAS! RIGHT NOW!" our mother yelled, waving her meat-covered hands around looking like a cross between a serial killer and a deranged windmill.

Unfortunately, at that age, my brothers were a lot better at demolition than construction and our father's entire tool cache consisted of a Swiss army knife. So the pile of redwood would remain just that, through the rest of the summer and the entire fall and winter. By the spring thaw, an extended family of mice had taken up residence and they seemed to be pretty content in their new digs. So I guess you could say that my brothers' handiwork did some good, after all.

Chapter 7

The Route 41 Outdoor Theatre

"IT LOOKS LIKE the rain has wrecked the flea market for today," the cabbie said.

"Huh? What didja say?" I responded.

Glancing out the cab window, I saw a big, open field with a large tent off to the side. A few people were entering the tent, but the parking area was nearly deserted.

"Heck," my driver said, "Most Saturday mornings, this place is jumpin'. Folks come here to get everything from soup fixin's and beautiful, classy velvet paintings to genuine imitation Rolexes."

Looking at his reflection in the rear view mirror, I watched him roll his eyes and let out a chuckle.

"Hey," I said. "Didn't this used to be that old drive-in movie theatre?"

"Yeah. It was the Starlight, I think. But me and my family went to the Route 41 'cause it was closer to where we lived," he added.

"Us too," I responded. Then I turned to gaze out the window once again.

Just over the Indiana border from the East Side was the local drive-in movie theatre. During the time in my life when the term "outdoor theatre" would mean a family outing, and long before becoming "the passion pit," the 41 Outdoor was one of our favorite weekend destinations.

Our folks would load the four of us into the backseat of the Ford in our pajamas with pillows and blankets and head to the outdoor movies. Once there, the old man rolled down his window and hung the heavy gray metal speaker from it. Rolling the window back up as far as possible in a futile attempt to reduce the impending mosquito invasion, our parents settled in for the previews of coming attractions.

In the meantime, my brothers and I headed to the small amusement area situated just below the big screen. It didn't matter that we were in our P.J.'s. So were all the other kids. It was at the 41 Outdoor that we were introduced to the early Disney favorites. Today, whenever I hear the song, "When You Wish Upon a Star," I can still smell the Buttercup Popcorn we'd spill in the car's backseat while vying for the best viewing position.

Some of the men who were parked with their families around us had obviously just come from their shift at the mill. Many faces that smiled as we passed still wore smudges of coal tar and their hair wore the telltale ridge created by hard hats. Yet, watching a cartoon of seven little men heading joyfully to their work in a sparkling diamond mine was a perfect, yet inexpensive way to be in another cleaner, more colorful place. At least for a little while.

As the movie started, we'd head back to the car from the playground. Jumping into the back seat, my brothers and I would plop our heads onto pillows and pull the light blankets up to our chins.

"I GOTTA GO PEE!"

"Me too!"

"Ah, fer chrissakes! Why the hell can't you kids ever get the urge before the damn movie starts?!" the old man griped. "Anybody that's gotta go, let's do it now. I'm not goin' back there again!"

It was always his job to take us up to the john, no matter what gender. So he'd roll down his window to hang the speaker back on its stand, letting in forty or fifty bloodthirsty mosquitoes, and trudge us up to the concession stand.

Once there, if I had to go, he would wait dutifully outside the ladies' restroom. Our father had mastered the technique of being able to hang around outside the women's john without looking like a pervert that just liked to do that sort of thing. While he waited, he'd try to keep a watchful eye on my brothers. Sometimes when he got distracted, calamity would strike, which was what happened this particular night.

"Aieeeeeeeeee! Helllp! I'm STUCK!"

The old man's attention snapped back to where he had last seen my brothers and, craning his neck in an attempt to peer through the crowd that had started to gather, he dismally realized what the commotion was.

Michael had stuck his arm up a cigarette vending machine in hopes of grabbing a pack of matches. My middle brother's fascination with fire was well-known. By the time our father had turned his attention back from the ladies' restroom door in response to the clamor, Michael was shoulder-deep into the machine.

"Sunnuvva… goddamn it Michael! How in the HELL did you…"

"WAAAAAA!"

"Ah, fer chrissakes, shaddup already. I'll get you out."

After fifteen minutes of attempting to extricate his son from the contraption, the old man realized that he might have to either steal the entire vending machine with Michael and his arm still in it, amputate Michael's arm with the Swiss army knife he always had handy or bite the bullet and ask for help. Wisely, he chose the last option.

Sprinting over to the concession stand, he sheepishly asked to see a manager.

A tall lanky kid came to the counter.

"Ahhhhh... heh heh... see, the kid there got kind of... ahh... his arm is up... ahhh."

The concession manager approached the machine carrying a large toolbox. Michael, mistaking the box for a doctor's bag, began to wail. He remembered that the last time he had encountered a doctor's bag, it had contained a large needle that hurt like hell. Back then, all any of us knew about doctors and their paraphernalia was what we learned from getting polio vaccinations. They left our arms aching for days. Most of us would've rather just gotten polio, even though we knew from TV that with polio, you could wind up in an iron lung. But, when we thought about it, an iron lung would probably get us out of going to school.

The old man tried to calm Michael while simultaneously groveling to the manager who had begun to dismantle the machine.

Within ten minutes, Michael was free. Our father bought a sausage pizza and Cokes from the concession stand while studiously avoiding eye contact with the clerk due to his embarrassment.

The old man shuffled us back to the car and herded us through the back door of the Ford while growling through clenched teeth, "Now I don't wanna hear another peep out of youse kids 'till the movie's over!"

We all made our regular racket as we tumbled into the back seat while shoving each other around to score the best spot.

"Would you kids knock it off? I can't hear the damn movie!" our mother raged. "And what the HELL took so long? I thought they just had to pee. I should've known I couldn't trust you guys to just go up and do your business and not waste a lot of time goofing around. Now, George, would you PLEASE go back and get me a 7-Up?!"

Chapter 8

Laugh Your Troubles Away

EVERY SUMMER, CHICAGO TV station WGN was saturated with commercials featuring local celebrity, Dick "Two Ton" Baker, his roly-poly torso jammed into an amusement park ride, guffawing and waving his arms wildly around while urging the viewing public to "Laugh your troubles away at Mad, Merry RIVERVIEW!"

If our parish carnival was a happy little blip in our summer activity schedule, Riverview was the major event. It was the Empire State Building compared to a pup tent. Mount Rushmore compared to the neighborhood landfill.

Once the first Two Ton Baker ad aired, my brothers and I would immediately start badgering our parents about the one outing we looked forward to with anticipation that made every occasion except Christmas pale in comparison. They usually managed to distract us with some lesser treat – a trip to the Tastee-Freez or a picnic at Eggers Grove, our local poison ivy-filled forest preserve. But they knew that inevitably they'd have to give in or listen to whining from September straight through fall and winter to the following June.

Photo used with permission from:
Chuck Wlodarczyk, author, "Riverview Gone But Not Forgotten"

Our trip to Riverview usually took place in mid to late August to soften the blow of the impending school year. By that time, the summer heat had become so oppressive that most days were spent sitting in the tepid water in our puny backyard pool. There was no shade, so by the end of the day, my brothers and I would head inside to have our sunburned faces, backs and shoulders slathered up by our mother with Noxzema skin cream. We were then bedded down in the living room on sheets in front of our family's one window air conditioner, since sleeping in our attic bedrooms was now unbearable.

The late summer misery was forgotten when the old man announced our annual pilgrimage to Riverview.

"Hold on to your hats, kids!" our father said with a grin. "Guess where we're goin' this weekend?" We knew that only one surprise could live up to his enthusiasm.

The park was a far cry from the sterile theme parks of today. Riverview was a Chicago fixture for decades and seemed to revel in its seamy splendor. It was always garishly reinventing itself, like an over-the-hill actress, grotesquely made up and obstinately refusing to settle into her role as fading vixen.

Aladdin's Castle was probably the most recognizable of the park's attractions. Most every article or book written about Riverview includes a picture of the turbaned Aladdin, with its enormous, dark eyes shifting, surveying his raunchy domain. The castle itself was a funhouse with distorted mirrors, rubber monsters behind wire cages (did the Riverview Board of Directors think these things would escape and run amok in the park?) and a rotating barrel, turned on its side so that you had to make it through to get out of the castle and back onto the midway. Just before the barrel was a short walkway featuring a sudden upward blast of air that blew female visitors' dresses up. This was open to the outside for the viewing pleasure of the usual throng of perverts who frequented the benches outside the funhouse.

Riverview had an impressive array of roller coasters, but The Bobs was the reigning king of the park's coaster collection. The construction was wood and the steady, blood curdling *clackety-clack clack* that the cars made on the coaster's track as they ascended to the first crest could never be duplicated in the steel framed coasters that followed. Riders were slammed into the cars' sides and each other as The Bobs shot its way through impossible twists and plunges. It was every guy's test of masculinity in front of his buddies or his girl.

A treasure chest full of personal artifacts supposedly found in the cars after rides was prominently displayed as a grim warning to all. Earrings, hats, false teeth, wigs, glass eyes – all gave pause to the unwary boarding The Bobs.

The Waterbugs were enormous inner tubes with small compartments on top that accommodated a single rider. The tube was then navigated around the Waterbug pool by its inhabitant, either into or away from fellow riders. The bugs were basically bumper cars on water, though the water was more viscid than liquid and glimmered with rainbow-hued gasoline slicks from the bobbing crafts. In addition, adding to its unique ambiance, the water surface always seemed to be studded with empty drink containers, grease and mustard-smeared food wrappers, along with other colorful, yet disgusting midway refuse.

The Chute-the-Chutes was a several stories tall ramp on which large gondolas, seating 20 or more, were launched down a wide slide into a moat. Guys bringing their dates to the park and familiar with the ride always suggested that the couple sit toward the back of the boat. Their clueless dates assumed it was so that they wouldn't get drenched when the gondola plunged into the water. The real reasoning was that the back of the boat would invariably get saturated, thus making the female partner's garb nearly transparent. The water that filled the Chute-the-Chutes moat was just as fetid as that upon which the Waterbugs bobbed. After disembarking, riders were left to deal with the dank, musty odor of sweat mixed with whatever it was that made the water opaque. The smell was so bad that most people just opted to burn their clothes later that day.

Looming over the park was the Parachute Jump, hoisting souls incredibly high up a wire to the pinnacle. If you had the guts to keep your eyes open, the view of the smoggy Chicago landscape was stupendous. Upon hitting the top, the chute would free fall for several dozen feet before opening and treating the riders to a lovely ride to the bottom, where you'd bounce a couple of times before the operator urged you to "C'MON! Get Off! Youse ain't the only ones that wanna ride! There's people waiting here!" He only directed these hollered instructions to kids, as teenagers and adults tended to be repeat riders.

One thing you'd find at some of the sleazier parks of that era was the Freak Show. Most years, our parents wouldn't let us go into the show. They were, while not holy-rollers, pretty sensitive to the plight of those less fortunate, like "The Lizard Boy." This was a young man with an unusually severe case of psoriasis that the creative folks who ran the attraction had washed over with a greenish coloring agent. Another popular freak show resident was "The Half Man" (an unfortunate guy who was normal from the torso up, but was attached to a large tire-like rubber appendage below). But the year that the Freak Show introduced "Popeye" – "He pops his eyes right out of his head!" – they had a hard time resisting the constant, insistent nagging of my brothers. Finally they gave in.

With a blessing from the old man, "This is complete bullshit, but if you wanna waste 50 cents, be my guest," we watched my brothers disappear through the tent flaps that blocked the freak show off from the non-paying public. I buried my face into the cotton candy I bought with part of the 50 cents I saved by not going in to view Popeye and the other freaks.

Our mother took this opportunity to meander over to a nearby booth to have her handwriting analyzed by "Mr. Omar." Mr. Omar had been a Riverview fixture for years and the highlight of our mother's day at the park was to watch with amazement as he reviewed her signature and related what an incredibly "intelligent, wise, and discerning" woman she was. "Honestly", he would add, "I have never seen such writing!" He'd ask her if she had "ever thought about going into politics? Or maybe the theatre?" Our mother would cast her eyes downward and smile, trying her best to look modest. She then brought the handwriting analysis back to the old man to prove what she had thought about herself all along.

Ten minutes later, the boys emerged from the show. Once George had cleaned himself of the puke Michael spewed his way when Popeye rolled his eyeballs completely out of his head and back in again, my brothers declared the show "Great! And really worth 50 cents! Even more!"

But our parents, observing the familiar, faraway look in Michael's eyes, were concerned. It was one thing to think of Michael earning his living with the juggling and sleight-of-hand tricks that he had perfected at our local church carnival and with which he continued to entertain neighbors and friends alike, for a small contribution. They figured that if he was persistent and lucky enough, he might wind up on the Ed Sullivan show. After all, the guy spinning plates on long sticks and the lady with the troupe of dogs wearing clown hats and jumping through hoops had nothing on Michael in the entertainment department.

It was quite another thing, however, to think of their middle son joining the ranks of folks like the bearded lady and JoJo the Dog-Faced Boy, leaving home forever to travel the world amidst wild animals and carny roustabouts.

Michael confided in me later that he had considered the monetary benefits of a talent like Popeye's. But the fear of never getting his eyeballs back into his head was the deciding factor.

"I'll find some kind of great job, though. There's no way I'm gonna be stuck in the mills," my brother vowed.

Chapter 9

Uncle Pat and the Slots

OUR HOUSE ON Greenbay Avenue had been formerly occupied by my maternal grandparents. When Grandma and Grandpa moved to Erie, PA to try their hand at mink ranching – one of many failed enterprises they embarked upon during more than 50 years of marriage – my mother and father decided that the bungalow had "good bones" and would be a fine place to raise a family.

My mother's sister, Aunt Dorothy, and her new husband, Uncle Pat Trella moved in with us so they could save money for their own place. Uncle Pat was Italian and his ways were unfamiliar and puzzling to the Polish/Russian contingent in our family. He cussed like a stevedore and made his own sausage that contained home grown basil and the homemade wine that he called "Dago Red." Uncle Pat's dark eyes and black wavy hair seemed exotic next to Aunt Dorothy's blond, blue-eyed beauty. His clothes were different from ours, too. For one thing, he wore unusual shoes. They were black loafers with large, white patches over the top. Never before, nor since have I seen anything like them. He often wore a tweed jacket or knit shirts that gave him a somewhat more urbane look than the rest of the East Side men who most often sported flannel or cotton.

From the beginning, the living arrangements were less than ideal. My mother and Aunt Dorothy fought incessantly. My mother used her new position as property overlord as an excuse to boss vassals Dorothy and Pat around. My father, a born pacifist, tried his best to stay out of the fray, lest my mother's wrath be directed at him. This led to a trickledown effect of heated arguments between Aunt Dorothy and Uncle Pat. They wanted out, but finances dictated otherwise.

Uncle Pat liked to take long, solitary weekend jaunts around the neighborhood. My aunt became suspicious of his ever-lengthening absences, so she suggested that it would be nice if Uncle Pat let me tag along. "You know, give the kid some fresh air, give mother a break", the usual phony excuses used to enlist the aid of a junior spy. Uncle Pat gave in easily. He told my aunt that he'd take me to Wolf Park, the grungy East Side playground.

So off we headed toward the park. As we walked, Uncle Pat would stop every once in a while to observe how the long, slender green pods of the Catalpa trees that laid strewn over the sidewalk would make great pretend swords or that they looked like something the Owl and the Pussycat could sail away on. When I pointed out several long yellow and black striped caterpillars on the tree's leaves, Uncle Pat explained that these worms, though they munched on the leaves of the trees, didn't hurt the Catalpa. But rather, they were greatly prized by fishermen (including him and my father) because their skin was tough and their flesh juicy and delicious, at least to the fish.

Uncle Pat & Aunt Dorothy

He pointed up to the spider web of electric and telephone lines that squirrels darted on from pole to pole. He asked me why I thought the squirrels liked these poles since they weren't known to produce acorns or walnuts.

"Ummm... maybe they like to be up there to stay away from dogs and cats?" I asked.

"Very good, Georgia!" my uncle responded. "I'll bet that's the reason!"

Uncle Pat had a way of gently urging me to think that made it seem like I was solving some great mysterious puzzle. Aside from a wide variety of talents that included cooking up the world's best spaghetti sauce, he was a wonderful teacher. My own personal Mister Wizard. And now, this marvelous person was taking me to the park! What a great day!

Three blocks later, we stood in front of the 9-foot high, green chain link fence that enclosed the park. Uncle Pat smiled down at my eager face. Then he grabbed my hand and made an abrupt turn to cross the street to our local VFW hall, which housed the neighborhood slot machine operation.

My disappointment soon gave way to excitement when I heard the whirs and bells, the hoots of the winners and cussing of the not-yet-winners. Uncle Pat, it would turn out, was a consistent not-yet-winner.

The air was thick with smoke and the yeasty smell of beer. From the corner of the large room, I heard somebody yell, "Seven, come Eleven!"

"Why did that guy yell those numbers, Uncle Pat?" I asked.

"They're playing a game, Georgia! With Dice! Ain't this fun?" my uncle said, with a grin.

As I held his hand and we walked through the place, a couple of the men clapped my uncle on the back and others shook his hand with greetings of "Hiya Pat! Good to see ya! Hey! Who's your pretty little girlfriend?" I beamed, proud to be with this obviously very popular guy.

He whispered, "I wanna show you somethin' Georgia!"

Oh boy! The last time Uncle Pat wanted to show me somethin' was when he did a trick taking off half his thumb and putting it back. It was one of the most interesting things I had seen in my short life.

But first, he took me to the concession stand, where he bought me a box of licorice flavored Pine Brothers cough drops – my favorite. They were strong-tasting, gummy and they stuck my back teeth together. As he handed me the box of Pine Brothers, Uncle Pat said, "We don't need to tell Aunty Dorty that we didn't go to the park. She's just happy that we went out for a little while... ok?" I guess he figured I'd be less likely to snitch if he gave me candy. Even if I had the urge to squeal, maybe my mouth would be stuck shut so long that I'd lose interest. Uncle Pat knew that his niece had the attention span of a gnat.

Then my uncle once again took my hand as we walked over to one of the big silver machines. They were set on wooden tables, and from my perspective all I could see was a rounded front with something long sticking up from the side. Uncle Pat reached in his pocket and pulled out a coin. He dropped it into a slot on the machine, then he lifted me up.

"Greeyab the heeyandle, Georgia Ayaynn!" he blurted in his heavy South Chicago accent. My uncle called me Georgia Ann when he was either very angry or very excited. He pulled me down while I held the lever.

"Now, let go!"

Then I was hoisted back up and my uncle gleefully shouted, "Watch for the cherries, Georgia Ayaynn!! Watch for the cherries!"

Cachunk. Cachunk. Cachunk. Three pictures came up. A bunch of cherries! Another bunch of cherries! And then... ooooooohhh. An orange.

Though he didn't say anything, Uncle Pat's disappointment was palpable. Slowly he lowered me to the floor. Then, his eyes lighting up, he said, "Well, haay-ell... let's try again!"

Once again, he lifted me up, and I clutched the lever. Down, then back up to watch the little pictures pop into the window.

This time, there were no matches. Undeterred and, remarkably, with even more enthusiasm than the last time, my uncle uttered what would become one of my favorite life phrases. "Three's a charm!" It wasn't.

As we walked home hand-in-hand, my uncle and me, he again asked me to please not worry Aunt Dorothy by telling her that we had never made it to Wolf Park. Then rather than pointing out the usual interesting observations about trees and squirrels, Uncle Pat shared his cherished dream with me.

"I can't give your Auntie Dorty so much right now, Georgia Ayann. But someday, when I win, honey, I'm gonna buy a coupla places somewhere nice for both our families. Wouldn't you like to look out your bedroom window at a pretty lake or a river or maybe the ocean?

The thought was so foreign to me, so totally out of the realm of my imagination he may as well have asked me if I wouldn't rather live on the moon than in our house on Greenbay. I said, "Mmmmmm… I guess so."

"Okay, Georgia, think about it, if you could live anywhere in the world, where would it be?"

"I think it'd be real nice to live at Disneyland!" I answered. "Then I could ride those flying Dumbos every day!"

Uncle Pat smiled down at me and squeezed my hand.

He said, "I guess for now you'd just be happy with more Pine Brothers cough drops, right?"

I said that was right. But I added that I thought living by a lake or at Disneyland sounded really nice.

The next year, Uncle Pat and Aunt Dorothy had a baby and moved to a place of their own. It was not by a lake or the ocean, but rather in Blue Island, which was not an island, nor was it blue.

All was not lost, however, as just about the time the Trellas moved out, the old man started working for our neighborhood bookie, which introduced my brothers and me to the Fair Elms Tap.

Chapter 10

Friday Nights at the Fair Elms

THE FAIR ELMS TAVERN on the corner of Greenbay Avenue was one of the places where our father delivered his weekly quota of football cards and picked up the bets placed by bar patrons in hopes that a Big Win might pay for that new window air conditioner, new tires for the car, or a trip to the Wisconsin Dells. He then delivered those bets back to Big Angelo Colucci, the neighborhood bookie.

We liked Big Angelo, or "Uncle Angelo", as he was known to the tavern patrons' kids, though we all knew we weren't related. We liked his wife Roxanne even more. She had pink hair and wore tight Capri pants with high-heeled, open-toed pumps, revealing bright fuchsia toenails. She would bring us the 45 rpm records from all the neighborhood taverns' jukeboxes when they were changed out. Roxanne always smelled like Juicy Fruit gum and always greeted us with "Hellooooo mah precious ones!" while rustling one kid's hair into a bird's nest.

The word "syndicate" was unknown to us kids. In those simpler times, the only thing close to something shady we were aware of was the couple of years running when Father John won the car raffle at the parish carnival. Besides, what could possibly be wrong with this "uncle" guy and his delicious smelling wife?

The Fair Elms was the old man's last stop on Fridays – football card betting night. My brothers and I would usually come along. It was the highlight of our week, and our mother's too, since it would get us, however briefly, out of her hair. Once there, we would be unloaded from the back seat of the Ford and herded through the front door of the Fair Elms, one of us whining about the wad of gum that somehow got stuck in his hair sometime during the last two hours in close quarters and another noting that it smelled like somebody had stepped in something dog related and was now tracking it all over the place.

Our father, tuning out the bedlam, handed each of us a bottle of Kayo chocolate drink and our choice of either a bag of fried pork rinds, or a red-hot pickled sausage from the jar at the end of the bar. We were then plopped into our customary spots in the sawdust on the floor in front of the jukebox where we joined the offspring of plant workers and their wives who sat at the bar elbow-to-elbow with our dad, knocking down a few boilermakers. I remember how the sweet aroma of one of the patron's pipe tobacco would just about cover the stench of stale beer and dirty ashtrays.

The Wurlitzer jukebox was our earliest, and by far most innocent, excursion into the land of the psychedelic. We sat mesmerized, eyes glazed, jaws slack. The luminescent rainbow of lights swirled seductively, drawing us in, while seemingly keeping time with the background tunes of Dean Martin crooning about the moon, pizza pie, and amore. If a couple at the bar got into a fight or one of the old men fell off a barstool, we paid no heed. We were transfixed.

The whole place had a magical other-worldly feeling. The ceaseless fires from the blast furnaces of Republic Steel across the street, filtering through the tavern's front window, opaque from year upon year of mill grime, bathed the inside of the Fair Elms in a warm, amber glow. That glow was further enhanced for our father by several bottles of Pabst Blue Ribbon and shots of Southern Comfort.

A night on the town

Sometimes, and these were the really great times, our mother would join him.

When she walked in the tavern door, a spark would light the Old man's eyes and he'd yell, "Hey Pete! Get the wife a highball, would'ja? And another round of Kayos for the kids there!"

We knew right then that it would be an outstanding night. No usual Friday at-home fare of potato pancakes and canned tuna. Not this night. We'd be staying for the weekly tavern fish fry. Heaping platters of perch, fresh out of the Lake, would be set before us, along with French fries, coleslaw and Italian bread slathered in butter. Raspberry Jell-O with pillows of whipped cream on top for dessert.

We smiled, my brothers and me, as our second round of Kayos arrived and the record on the jukebox changed to our mother's favorite, Patti Page, asking the price of the doggie in the window.

And our father smiled, too, glancing sideways and winking at our mother. His girl. The lady he called Toots.

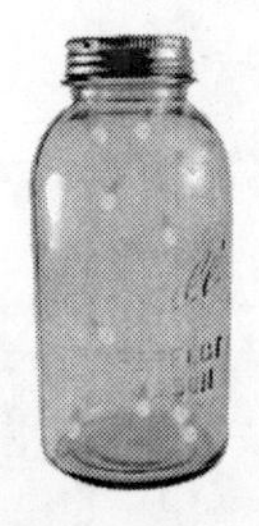

Chapter 11

My Mother, Politics, and a Pedigreed Dog

HER NAME WAS ANNIE. Nobody ever called my mother Ann or even Anna, her given name. She was Annie – a headstrong, pugnacious, visionary woman who could see right through a lie. I best remember her with a cloud of Tarreyton cigarette smoke haloing her head, sipping a cup of strong black coffee, her eyes glued to the TV screen, arguing with whatever politician was "politicking" at the time. Arguing. With a politician on TV. Those times, if the guy was, in her opinion, particularly dim-witted or duplicitous or if he had something to do with "Big Business," my mother would haul out her fantastic repertoire of Polish cuss words. When I asked once for a translation of an oft-repeated phrase, she mumbled something that had to do with a dog's blood and eternal damnation. I never asked again.

She realized, of course, that arguing with someone who could neither see, nor hear her was futile, so she would call his

Above left:
Mom at 19 years old

Above right:
Tippy

Right:
Mom in boat

office to "tell him a thing or two." Naturally, she never managed to get through, so my mother would follow up with a strongly worded letter. Or, if her need to set him straight was time-sensitive, as before an election or when tax increases were looming, she sent a telegram, asking point-blank just what in the hell he thought he was doing! If she were here today, Annie's name would be at the top of every local, state and federal list of subversives.

But my mother wasn't only about politics. Though she grew up during the Great Depression, my mom pictured a much different life for herself. In her mind, she was the neighborhood socialite and fashion diva. The mental picture didn't quite jibe with the woman we knew who hung laundry on the backyard line, often ankle-deep in the manure our father dumped in the yard yearly, hoping to create the carpet-like lawn he would never achieve.

One summer, when our family took its annual vacation to visit my maternal grandparents in Erie, PA, we returned home with a new pet. After Grandma and Grandpa's mink ranch went belly-up, they opened a tiny gas station and bought a small cluster of cottages they rented out. The gas station never made much money, but Grandpa and his youngest daughter, Carol, who was the gas pumper in chief, were accumulating a record-breaking collection of gas caps that they kept forgetting to replace after pumping fuel.

The folks who inhabited the cottages were an odd lot. Two were occupied by Grandpa's buddies who came over with him on the boat from Russia. They spent most of their time drinking vodka and staggering around grandpa's garden. The rest were an assortment of single moms, young families just starting out and, in one case, a dog breeder.

The breeder and his wife, Henry and Lillian Lillard, raised Bedlington terriers – an obscure English breed with a silver-grey, wooly coat. They resembled small sheep. I believe they were originally bred for some kind of hunting. In the case of our dog, whose pedigreed name was "Lillard's Blue Tip of Bo Peep," otherwise known as "Tippy," he seemed to have a genetic predisposition for biting humans and chasing garbage trucks and other assorted vehicles. I guess maybe that's because there weren't many fox hunts on the East Side.

When we were growing up, nobody we knew had a pedigreed dog. Most of the canines around our neighborhood were a nondescript mix of collie-shepherd-and-two-or-three-something-else's. So when we arrived back home with our new pet, my mother envisioned the hit she would make walking Lillard's Blue Tip of Bo Peep down the block in the red sheath dress she planned to buy, with a red leash and rhinestone-studded collar sported by the presumably beautifully behaved Tippy who would trot along beside her. I still can't figure out who my mother thought she was going to impress, since most of our neighbors worked all day and after dark, they would probably just take a look at my mother and wonder why in the world she would be all gussied up, walking down the block with a foreign-looking dog who was equally decked out.

The dress, leash and collar never materialized. Neither did the well-behaved dog. Tippy became adept at digging holes under our backyard fence and running amok in the neighborhood, terrorizing kids, mailmen and the other neighborhood pets. He wasn't selective about his prey. He was a bully dog, dressed in the deceptive wrapping of a little toy lamb.

Several times during Tippy's year-long tenure at our house, we would answer the doorbell and face a policeman who had brought him back. Why they never just took him to the pound is beyond me. Sometimes, I think they actually enjoyed seeing the disheartened look on our faces.

My parents bought him horsemeat from a specialty pet shop. Tippy dined like British canine royalty, while the rest of us ate macaroni and cheese and fried bologna sandwiches.

One day, shortly after Tippy had escaped our yard yet again, a mill worker who was driving by stopped and knocked on our door. He wondered if the beautiful Bedlington terrier who had chased his car belonged to us. Quickly checking the guy's arms for teeth marks and seeing none, our relieved mother answered in the affirmative. The mill worker explained that his family had owned a Bedlington when he was growing up and wondered if Tippy was for sale.

Barely able to contain her excitement, our mother held up her index finger signaling the guy to wait just a minute, ran into the kitchen, grabbed a package of uneaten horsemeat from the refrigerator, as well as the dog's barely used leash from a

Above:
Mink Ranch

Left:
Grandma and Grandpa

hook behind the door and ran to the front stoop before Tippy had a chance to show his true colors. As she handed the items to Tippy's new master, he nervously asked, "How much?" Our mother immediately responded, "Fifty bucks." Even at that time, the guy must've realized that it was a small amount for a dog with Tippy's obviously fine lineage.

Pulling a wad of bills out of his pocket, he counted them out. They were all ones and the wad amounted to eleven dollars. He apologized that he didn't have all the cash just then, but promised to stop by in the next day or two to pay for his new acquisition. Our mother snatched the bills from his hand and said that he could stop by with the rest of the payment whenever he had a chance. As the guy repeatedly offered thanks for her trust and assurances that Tippy would have a nice home, our mother placed a hand on his shoulder and, while responding with, "Yeah, yeah, that's fine... ok", she maneuvered him toward, then out the front door. He opened his mouth to say something else, but before he could, she shut the door in his face. She then turned around and leaned back against the door with closed eyes and a relieved smile. It wasn't until the car had pulled away that our mother realized that she had taken neither the guy's phone number, nor any other information, so we never saw the mill worker or Tippy ever again.

My brothers and I stood at the front window and watched as the car containing our dog disappeared down Greenbay Avenue. We weren't sorry to see him go, although having a pedigreed dog, even a loser one like Tippy, gave us a certain false air of exclusiveness.

The old man, upon hearing the news and after months of seeing winged dollar signs fly by as each new package of horsemeat was devoured by our pet, broke into an enormous grin. He put his arm around our mother and gave her a big squeeze.

Our mother, however, seeing her one chance to be the envy of the neighborhood going away with Lillard's Blue Tip of Bo

Peep, escaped our father's hug. Heaving a sigh of resignation and clad in her usual housedress, Annie went out to our backyard to hang clothes on a line under a sooty sky.

Injun Summer Picture

By John T. McCutcheon

"Yep, sonny, this is sure enough Injun Summer. Don't know what that is, I reckon, do you? Well, that's when all the homesick Injuns come back to play...Don't be skeered....hain't none around here now, leastways no live ones..."

"Jever notice how the leaves turn red 'bout this time 'o year? That's jest another sign 'o redskins. That's when an old Injun sperrit gits tired dancin' and goes up and' squats on a leaf t-rest....See here's one now. See how red it is? That's the war paint rubbed off'n an Injun ghost, sure's you're born."

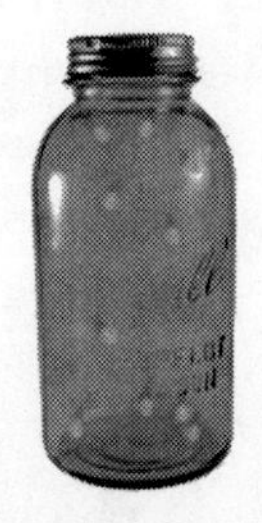

Chapter 12

Injun Summer

EVERY AUTUMN, AN iconic cartoon appeared on the front page of the Sunday supplement to *The Chicago Tribune.* In it were two frames of an old man and his grandson looking over a field of corn shocks with a small pile of embers burning in the foreground. The first frame was in red-orange and golden hues. The old man, puffing his pipe, sits on a log and spins a tale of dancing Indians. The second frame transforms the golden field into deep indigo blues with corn shocks becoming teepees and Indian revelers, outlined in black against a hazy harvest moon.

Once summer was over, our attention turned toward school and figuring out the best way to bluff our way through the year without actually learning anything. The nuns, however, had another agenda. They viewed their charges, perhaps realistically, as a pack of losers. They also felt that it was their duty to do the best they could with us. Historically, the first day of school was spent with the good sisters eyeballing their classes, picking out any potential troublemakers and basing their disciplinary measures for the coming school year accordingly. This was usually accomplished by gut feeling, but sometimes, in the case of the Nejak family, the current pupil's resemblance to some members of the nun's past classes played a distinct role.

Our youngest brother, Joey, arrived for first grade all bright-eyed and hopeful and made his mark by joyfully swinging on the volleyball net in the schoolyard. The first-grade nun, either seeing or sensing a playground transgression, barreled down the schoolyard with her habit billowing in the breeze. As she screeched to a halt in front of the bunch of kids gathered around the little boy merrily bouncing in the net, her eyes narrowed in recognition.

"Ahhhhhh... You're a *Nejak,* aren't you?"

Joey, innocently unaware of the fate that awaited him, proudly admitted that he was, in fact, a Nejak. This simple statement sealed his fate with his new teacher. Due to past transgressions committed by his older siblings, Joey was now found guilty by association. His new teacher would henceforth look at all his actions with a jaundiced eye. He was screwed, but at the time, he didn't realize it.

Despite the dismal fact that autumn heralded our return to school, the season brought with it the promise of crisp nights, the earthy, intoxicating aroma of burning leaves and Halloween.

The Halloween pumpkin was chosen by our old man with the single-minded zeal of someone choosing a bride for his first-born son. When he got the gourd home, he'd core open the top and plunge up to his elbows into pumpkin guts. We'd watch and shudder, along with our mother, as he pulled out fistfuls of orange slime, plopping it into a bowl and suggesting to our mother that she separate the slime from the seeds and salt and bake them, so that we'd have "a nice snack" later on.

With regard to our trick-or-treating garb, our parents, never ones to follow the crowd, didn't succumb to our whines about the latest costumes available at Woolworths. Whether it was their latent creativity kicking in or the lack of funds needed for a store-bought costume, they always came up with the perfect theme for our Halloween revelry.

The old man was an artistic genius in the medium of burnt cork. When we asked what we would be for Halloween, his answer was always, "BUMS, of course!"

So the four of us would head out into the brisk twilight, sporting beards, sideburns, moustaches, heavy black eyebrows and dragging empty, worn pillow cases (much more resilient than paper bags) to collect our share of the neighborhood bounty. We were accompanied by our friends, many of them bums, as well, with a couple of ghosts (sheet over the head with eye holes cut out) thrown in. There weren't many ghosts, though, as bed sheets were a valuable commodity and, unless they were completely unsalvageable, were considered much too precious to be used for such a frivolous purpose. Others, especially the kids from the upper crust part of the East Side were magnificently arrayed in their store-bought princess, super hero and monster costumes.

A couple of hours later, we'd arrive home dragging behind our sacks full of popcorn balls, pennies, those orange and black wrapped peanut butter things and some Hershey kisses that looked to be leftover from the previous Christmas. No matter. We were ready to dig in, but first, our mother whipped out the Noxzema jar – the same one she had used to soothe our sunburn a few months earlier – and attempted to scrub off the old man's exuberant burnt cork artwork. We would emerge from the bathroom, faces pink and shiny, ready to dig into our plunder.

Not so fast. First, we had to pay a visit to Chef Boyardee. We had completely forgotten that we hadn't eaten dinner before heading out on our Halloween forage.

I hated Chef Boyardee. After living with Uncle Pat Trella and enjoying his homemade spaghetti sauce, the Chef's recipe seemed insipid, at best.

But if that was the price we had to pay to get to the good stuff, well, bring it on. Actually, the pale red sauce and bird-dropping like hints of meat didn't taste so bad some nights, especially if you sprinkled on enough of the parmesan sawdust that came in the package. In the 1950's, when processed foods began showing up, in order to make a meal from a package, certain steps had to be taken. And the 1950's homemakers didn't mind. After all, if the noodles were separate from the sauce and then you had to add cheese, well, isn't that pretty close to homemade? Years later, when I introduced my own kids to the Chef, his recipe, which now came pre-mixed in a can, seemed downright unbeatable.

Chapter 13

The Day I Ate My Noodles

BEFORE STARTING grade school, the image I had of nuns was of sweet-faced earth angels in peculiar headgear who lived for the joy of ringing chimes, singing pretty hymns, and smiling benignly at the children entrusted to their daily care and teaching. That image had been formed over years of watching Bing Crosby movies. Whoever produced those films had obviously never attended a Catholic grade school.

The nuns of our parish school made Uncle Charlie the ice cream man's hatred of kids look like a love fest. My fellow pupils and I were absolutely certain that when they weren't sucking up to the priests, the nuns spent their off work hours devising fiendish schemes to make the hours we spent in class some of the most miserable of our short lives.

No transgression went unnoticed. And none were so small that they didn't incur the sisters' wrath. Corporal punishment was doled out generously and with delight.

Most lessons, no matter what the subject, were given a religious slant. If it was math, we were reminded that the number three was indicative of the three Persons in the Holy Trinity. If it was science, well, God was behind everything. Even English lessons took on a convoluted spiritual connotation, where words like "miracle" and "sacrament" were slipped into our spelling bees among all the "transgressions" and "dynasties."

Fearing the nuns as I had never feared anybody, I tried to be invisible. I didn't do too well during my first few years in school, mainly because my eyesight was so poor that I couldn't see the blackboard. My third grade teacher, a nun whose very name struck terror into the hearts of pupils both past and present, was the bane of the school's student population. We never knew in advance which class would be stuck with her, and it's probably a good thing since foreknowledge of being one of her pupils would've undoubtedly triggered an extremely youthful dropout population.

Sister was four feet ten, even in her clunky two-inch heeled, lace-up oxfords. And she was pure muscle. In the morning, as we heard the rosary beads that hung from her waist rattling down the hall toward our classroom, along with the heavy stomp-stomping of her shoes, our blood ran cold.

The nun had decided at the beginning of the school year that I was a complete burnout, so she stuck me in the back row of the classroom – affectionately known as the "slow row." The kids in the slow row weren't ever called on, as we were never expected to know the right answer. Since I could barely see the blackboard from the front row, once I had been relocated to the back of the class, the blackboard and its lessons became nothing but a vague blur and distant memory. I and my fellow back-row buddies may as well have been in a totally different school or planet as far as Sister was concerned.

One day, the nun jotted some notes on the blackboard. The words read, "Yellow equals three, blue equals four, red equals five," and so on. She listed about a dozen different colors, all with numerical values. Of course, she could have been writing the instructions for building a nuclear bomb and I wouldn't have known the difference. I couldn't see a thing.

As I lazily scribbled on my yellow lined pad, Sister passed out colored macaroni from a shoebox. There were yellow rigatoni, green bow ties, blue elbow macaroni – a kaleidoscope of brightly-dyed pasta on our desks. It was to be our math lesson. However, not being able to read the blackboard, I naively thought they were a treat. As much as I disliked and feared the nun, I felt kind of sorry for the old bat. "Poor Sister," I thought. She's trying to give us a treat, however lame, and the other kids are being mean.

So one by one, I popped the colored pasta into my mouth. They were a little hard to get down, even though I chewed them up pretty well before swallowing. One by one, my classmates turned around to see what the racket was coming from my desk.

The nun, following the stares of the class, as well as the puzzling crunching noises coming from the slow row, strode over to me, hands on hips, rosary beads jangling.

"MISS NEJAK! WHERE ARE YOUR NOODLES?!"

Beaming up at her, I replied "Thanks, S'tr! They were real good!"

"CAN'T YOU READ THE BLACKBOARD?"

"Uhhhhhh..."

I squinted hard at the blackboard and desperately acted like I was trying to pronounce something that I couldn't even see. I thought if I showed her I was making an effort, then she might be a little happier.

But a happy demeanor wasn't in the nun's realm of emotion.

"Hmmmmmmph. I see," she muttered.

That night at home, the phone rang. I heard my mother talking in hushed tones, but when I caught the words, "I don't understand, Sister... she never said anything about not being able to see", my ears perked up.

When she put the receiver down, my mother folded her arms as she always did before delivering a lecture.

"So, why didn't you TELL me that you couldn't see?"

But I *could* see, I thought. I was looking right at her, after all.

"Ach… you make me crazy. You know that?" my mother said.

A week later, I showed up to class sporting a pair of glasses with blue plastic frames embedded with silver glitter. The glass-

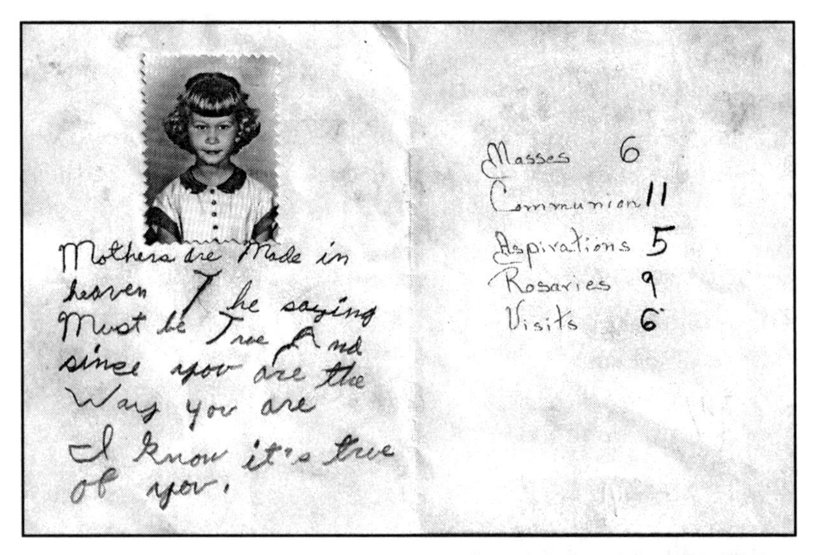

Above:
Mother's Day Card

Right:
First Communion Day

es proved helpful and week after week, I migrated closer to the front row, thoroughly enjoying my newfound academic progress. I made a solemn vow right then that never would I ever look down upon anyone who, for whatever reason, was banished to the slow row whether in school or in life.

The change in my abilities, however, did little to assuage the nun's (or my fellow student's) view of me. This, I feel, was mainly due to my aroma. Our Catholic school had a uniform policy for the girls of dark blue gabardine – a material known for its inability to "breathe". The combination of color and tight weave encouraged the body to produce enormous quantities of sweat, even during the cooler months. I was a pretty sweaty kid, especially for a girl, and it didn't help that my mom thought that all deodorant was poisonous. Also, the meals my mother prepared were conglomerations of delicious, yet pungent ingredients like sauerkraut, garlic, onions and smelly cheeses – all of which tended to exude from the pores of the consumer for days. Whereas most of the girls in my class wore scents of lilacs and Sweetheart soap, I always smelled like a simmering pot of vegetable soup.

Consequently, my classmates formed little groups around the perimeters of the classroom to avoid the noxious fumes that radiated from around my desk. For a while, I was able to deflect blame away from myself and onto the nun. My desk was now close to the front, and when my fellow pupils began to notice the unusual smell up there, I acted clueless while once in a while casting a disdainful eye at Sister. But when she stepped out and the odor stayed behind, all eyes fell on me. That probably accounts for my adult obsession with deodorant soaps, sprays, gels, powders and sticks.

If I die of an unnatural cause, it'll probably be Lady Mitchum syndrome.

At least then, my mother with her deodophobia will finally be vindicated.

Chapter 14

Fatherly Visits and Zulu Boys

EVERY COUPLE OF months, the school Pastor, Father John, would make the rounds visiting each classroom in the school. Prior to his visit, the nuns would go completely off their collective rockers, even further off than usual.

In an effort to impress him, they'd whip us into a frenzy of activity. We pasted multi-colored glitter on construction paper Ave Maria's to be stapled to the corkboard that surrounded the classroom. We learned the words to obscure hymns, each nun frantically searching the books for ever more off-the-wall examples, not to be outdone by her rival sisters. We were coerced into cramming the Zulu Boy bank with all our spare change. The bank was a shoebox-sized, metal container with a little black boy on the top, hands folded in prayer, and a bobble head that only moved when coins were dropped in the slot. Supposedly, the money we dropped in would help the missionaries trying to convert all the pagans over in Zululand. I had no idea where Zululand was, but I figured it must be somewhere around Russia, as everybody knew Russia was loaded with Godless Communists. And, it seemed reasonable that God would want to keep all the heathens rounded up in one place so that they'd be easier to keep track of.

Most times, the nuns were allied with one another against us, a tight-knit community, nuns vs. pupils. They never seemed to look at us as anything other than annoying roadblocks in their path to heaven. But in the days before a pastoral visit, we always reached an uneasy truce.

The day the priest arrived, whichever sister was in charge of our class that year would suddenly radiate a strange combination of beatific joy and blissful peace. It was scary, since just a couple of days before, that same nun was a human cyclone of unbridled rage, whose only source of joy seemed to be the infliction of fear and pain. But we always welcomed the respite from the norm. And each time, we naively hoped that the transformation was more than temporary.

When Father John finally swept into our classroom, the nun would clap twice and we'd all stand.

"Children, what would you like to say to Father?!"

"Goooood morrrnnniiiing Faaaaaather Johhhhhn!" we'd sing-song.

"Good morning to you, boys and girls! You're all looking very well today! Bless you all!" he gushed.

"Now you may be seated!"

Then, clasping his hands behind his back, his large belly preceding him, Father John sauntered around the room admiring the spelling tests, penmanship lessons and religion-themed crayon drawings lining the walls, all sporting gold or silver stars.

Nerve jangling though these visits could be, we much preferred encountering the priest in this context rather than in the confessional. You could always tell which booth contained Father John by the short line. Grade schoolers didn't usually have much to confess – there was the usual "disobeyed my parents," or "lied to sister about my homework." Probably the worst transgression was "snatched a candy bar from the drug store." But no matter. Father John's baritone would boom out, "YOU

DID WHAT?!" He would then follow up with a loud lecture on what it meant to be a good young Catholic. After all, he scolded us, if we didn't "set a fine example for the public school kids," who would? He would then dole out some elaborate penance – fifty Hail Mary's, forty-five or so Glory Be's, a couple dozen Our Fathers, self-flagellation, a trip to Lourdes.

The chastised confessional occupant would slink out of the booth red-faced, vowing next time to either avoid Father John's confessional altogether or lie. The latter would practically guarantee you an eternity in hell, but at the time, it was better than facing the wrath of Father John.

Next on the pastoral visit agenda, our class would stand and warble whatever hymn the nun had settled on, which we'd usually screw up since it wasn't ever one we were familiar with. Amazingly, though words and notes were missed and butchered, the good sister smiled through it all. At least, her lips were smiling... we couldn't read the expression that glared behind the wire rimmed glasses. The priest would then pick up the Zulu Boy bank and give it an appreciative shake, admiring its heft. Then he was off to the next classroom and we would heave a collective sigh of relief.

Or not. Sister wasn't smiling anymore. Grim faced and muttering to herself, the nun's narrowed eyes scanned the room for whoever she imagined had "acted up" during the visit. Gone was the beatific air of peace and love. We were back to smack first and ask questions later.

Clomp, clomp. Jangle, jangle. Eyes squeezed shut, we listened, terrified, as the familiar "nun on the move" sounds traveled around the room. Where would she stop? The sounds got louder, then... *OH NO!* She stopped next to my desk!

Quaking in my seat, I slowly opened my eyes and glanced to the side. Whew! Her back facing me, the nun let loose on her chosen victim with a verbal tirade.

"MR. KOZOWSKI! I SAW YOU SMIRKING WHEN WE SANG OUR SONG FOR FATHER! DID YOU THINK THE SONG WAS FUNNY?!"

"No, S'tir," James Kozowski mumbled, morosely.

He knew from experience what was coming.

"Then why don't you tell the class why you were smirking, Mr. Kozowski?" the nun's voice dripped with sarcasm.

"Ummmmm... I... uhhhhhhhh," James stuttered.

"HAH! I thought so!"

WHACK!

The nuns could be very creative in their instruments of punishment, as well as targeted body parts. Rubber-tipped pointer sticks were a favorite, as they could reach across several innocent students to reach the knuckles of her current target. Blackboard erasers frequently went airborne as a nun winged it across an entire classroom to bonk the head of anyone suspected of not paying sufficient attention to the current subject. Their aim was incredible. I used to imagine how much the White Sox would have valued an arm like that.

But nothing struck fear into our hearts like the sight of one of the nuns, jaw set, empty handed, zeroing in on the ears of an unsuspecting victim. Ears were especially handy when someone sat right next to the blackboard, as they could be used as handles to bang the head sharply against the board.

We never dared report these antics to our parents. They knew firsthand how awful we could be, so Sister must be right, they would reason. Either that or for all the time we've lived with them since birth, we must've had them buffaloed into not seeing our true nature. That's it, they'd reason, the good nuns have simply discovered the real us. In any case, the score was always nuns 1 – kids 0.

And so went the old Catholic elementary school routine. We did learn a lot, but it came with a heavy price. Any violation of the nuns' idea of proper behavior was dealt with swiftly and painfully. And scholastics were tempered with moral lessons at every turn. Basically, if something was fun or even borderline enjoyable, it was probably a sin.

This premise was drummed into our young, open minds day after day, month after month, eon after eon. The nuns went to great lengths to remind us that no matter how good we tried to be, we were still plenty rotten and could probably look forward to a couple of centuries in Purgatory, a Catholic invention meaning temporary hell.

After years miserably spent in the company of the nuns, however, we all figured that if condemned to Purgatory, we should at least be given a lighter sentence for time already served.

Chapter 15

Merry Christmas To All

THE CHRISTMAS OUR dad bought the Polaroid Land Camera was one of the most memorable in my immediate family history. In retrospect, it was one of the best, despite the fact that the one material thing we coveted most that year would soon be lost forever.

The old man had started saving for the camera, brand new on the market, in July. Every payday, any cash not spent on bills, food and other necessities, was put in our father's camera fund jar. In those innocent times of early technology, the thought of taking a picture and watching it develop before our dazzled eyes made his heart quicken. And at Christmas, our father was a bigger kid than any of us.

Every year, our Christmas tree was the envy of the neighborhood and our extended family – at least to those who hadn't succumbed to the aluminum or flocked tree crazes popular at the time. One of our neighbors even had a tree that appeared to be constructed entirely of white plastic fluff, studded with pink and lavender mercury glass bulbs. The tree basked in the glow of a revolving color wheel, changing it from white to silver, then gold. It was splendidly displayed in the picture window of one of the only newer, blond brick bi-level homes in our neighborhood of dreary brown bungalows.

"Did you see that white tree down the block? It's beautiful! Can we get one just like that?" I pleaded.

"Are you nuts? That thing is an insult to Christmas!" my father scolded. "The only way that plastic monstrosity would smell like the holiday is if they soaked it in spruce juice! And then you'd hafta keep your eyes shut to look at it!" The old man was Mr. Traditional Holiday Guy.

Right after Thanksgiving, our family would hit the tree lots, looking for a tree worthy of our father's decorating zeal. Sometimes we would luck out and find a suitable one the first time out. More often, it would take two or three trips before the old man would spot the perfect specimen. For a while, he was on a Scotch pine kick. He liked the long, silky needles and the trees were always full and well-shaped. But his all-time favorite was the Frasier fir, whose small needles and multi-armed branches afforded a better background for his artistry. Unfortunately, as with many cases of love at first sight, his instant attraction would sometimes ignore common sense. This would result in us getting the tree home and realizing that a foot or two would need to be lopped off in order for it to clear our ceiling. No matter – it was his diamond in the rough, and he intended to polish it to multi-carat perfection.

First came the lights. In the years before Italian lights became the rage, we had the usual teardrop-shaped bulbs, along with candle lamps containing an oil, which, when heated, bubbled like molten honey.

Next came the draping of the tinsel. It was this step, ritually performed year after year, that made the old man's trees so outstanding. As kids we were only allowed to tinsel the back of the tree. The front belonged to our father, and he worked in tinsel like Rembrandt worked in oils. 1950's era tinsel was heavy, and hung straight down. Never did he allow the tinsel to hit a lower

Dad decorating tree

One Christmas morning

Our Dad's Masterpiece

branch. Each strand was put on meticulously, with as many as fifty shining strands to a single branch. During this process, he'd have the tree lights glowing, so that he could judge the effect as he progressed.

While we worked on our evergreen masterpiece, the smells of Polish sausage and sauerkraut, ham, pierogies frying in butter and onions and walnut rolls in the oven would waft in from the kitchen. That was our mother's domain and she ruled it well.

Every couple of minutes, as we stood back from the tree to assess our progress, our father would remark that "This'll make a great picture! I can't wait to pick up that camera!"

Finally, it was Christmas Eve and our street was blanketed in fresh snow. The full moon and street lamps sprinkled the landscape with what looked to us to be stardust.

The old man headed out to get his camera, which had been on layaway since the beginning of November. Once my brothers and I had taken our baths and put on our flannel pajamas, we joined our mother in front of the glowing tree to watch "A Christmas Carol" and await our dad's return.

An hour-and-a-half later, he came home. He was pale and looked like he had aged ten years since he had left. Taking our mother's hand, our father led her into the kitchen. His normally strong voice broke as he explained that when he picked up our new Polaroid camera, he put it on the roof of the Ford while fishing for the car keys. He then drove to our uncle's house to show off his new toy before returning home. Upon arrival, he realized that the camera wasn't on the seat beside him. Panic stricken, he mentally retraced his steps and realized what had happened. Rushing back to the now-closed store, our father searched the parking space, the street, and sidewalk, hoping against hope that the Polaroid would still be there.

It wasn't.

Then our mother spoke. While we couldn't hear every word, certain phrases stood out. "George… was just a camera. We'll save… another one. Christmas… all together… healthy… what really matters." Our mother's gentler side always seemed to come out when her heart overtook her usual orneriness.

Our mother and father came out of the kitchen hand-in-hand. She said, "Your father accidentally lost the camera, but that's ok... we'll save up for another one. In the meantime, let's take some pictures! She went to the closet in their room and got out the old Brownie Starflash. While our dad took pictures of the tree and my brothers and me, our mother went back to the kitchen. She came out with a hot toddy for our dad and one for herself. Leaving the room again, she returned with a tray holding four cups of hot cocoa and a plate of walnut roll slices and red and green sprinkled sugar cookies.

An hour later, my brothers and I were tucked in bed to await the arrival of Santa Claus.

The next morning, as the first real blizzard of the winter covered our town with several more inches of snow, our parents cuddled on the floral-printed couch with their arms around each other.

My brothers and I sat on the floor amidst our new treasures. I had asked for an enormous stuffed gorilla, but Santa, in his wisdom, brought me a junior chemistry set, complete with microscope. It was ok, though. Stuff looked fascinating under a microscope. I saw it on Mr. Wizard. I couldn't wait to examine samples of bugs. And leaves. And boogers. George and Michael were fighting imaginary Indians from their new Fort Apache play set. Joey had gotten a hamster, complete with cage and running wheel. He had taken his new pet out of the cage to teach him some tricks and the rodent immediately made a break for freedom. It would be weeks before we'd find him in a kitchen cabinet in a nest he had constructed out of shredded newspapers and candy wrappers, enjoying the stash of cereal and crumbs he had stockpiled.

The photos we took that year with the old Brownie still exist. Our tree in those old photos looked like a bejeweled pyramid – one of the finest we had ever decorated. We would eventually get a Polaroid Land Camera. Like so many other things, the pictures taken with the Polaroid have long since faded into oblivion.

Chapter 16

Mouseketeer Dreams and Miss Vicki's School of the Dance.

IF ANYONE HAD asked me in my early years what I wanted to be when I grew up, I would have been at a loss to answer. I never thought that far ahead. My only aspiration as a kid, the one thing I lusted after more than anything else, was to be a Mouseketeer.

Every day after school, I'd plant myself on the floor in front of our enormous console TV with the miniscule screen to watch Annette, Bobby, Karen and Cubby and the rest of the mouse crew tap dance, sing and generally ham it up. They seemed to be having such a great time. My forte at the time was not so much the dancing, but I knew every single word to every Club song. I could just imagine how impressed the Mouseketeers would be with me when they learned this. These kids, though they were on TV and I was in my living room, were my friends and I was theirs. Kindred spirits that had just not yet connected. Also, I figured that joining the Mickey Mouse Club talent pool was my way up and out of the dregs of the East Side.

I knew that the chance of either Walt Disney, head Mouseketeer, Jimmy Dodd, or any of the Disney talent scouts coming to our neighborhood to conduct auditions were slim to none – unless they found out there was rare, undiscovered talent there.

So I decided to improve my chances by badgering my mother until she enrolled me in Miss Vicky's School of the Dance, the East Side's premier and only dance class. The school was located in a dusty one-room studio above a shoe store on 106th and Ewing, smack dab in the middle of our major neighborhood shopping district.

Miss Vicky was a middle-aged diva with an enormous pot belly and equally large butt. She squeezed her ample figure into dazzling sequined leotards with matching tights that were at least two sizes too small. Her bleach blond hair was pulled back into a tight bun, accentuating her black and gray roots. Her expressions were, for the most part, dour and she barked out orders like a drill sergeant. Thinking back, I suppose that Miss Vicky resented being stuck in that studio, trying to teach the art of the dance to a brood of bumbling, talentless wretches when, in her mind, she should be dancing the lead role in Swan Lake at the Met.

Actually, some of us were worse than others. Some, meaning me. This was probably because I spent all my time in dance class ignoring instructions and daydreaming about being fitted for my pleated skirt, tee shirt emblazoned with my "Georgia" logo and red-bowed mouse ears. When I did actually try to get into the routine, I invariably spun and lurched in the opposite direction of my dance class mates, smashing into the rest of the troupe and raising Miss Vicki's blood pressure by double digits.

After two months of classes, during which I never managed to master even the most basic tap or ballet moves, Miss Vicky was at her wit's end. Also, our first recital was just a few weeks away and she feared that, barring any sudden and unlikely improvement, I would ruin the whole group's routine.

So one day after school as I sat mesmerized in front of the TV, chanting along with my Mouse Club friends, "Saddle your pony, here we go. Down to the talent Ro-de-o. Come along Sally, Jim and Joe – Join the talent round up!" my mother came up from behind and tapped me on the shoulder. She had a Hostess Snowball on a plate and was wearing an overly cheerful expression, one usually reserved for delivering especially unpleasant news. Also, since my mom usually didn't interrupt my daily viewing ritual, let alone with my favorite dessert before supper, I knew it must be something important.

Suddenly, the cheerful expression disappeared. My mother seemed to be wrestling with two conflicting emotions. Then she let me have it.

"You know, Georgia, I asked you if you were gonna knuckle down and apply yourself to this dancing school stuff. How many times have you started something and not followed through? First, there was Girl Scouts. We bought you the uniform, paid to send you away to that damn camp and all you got out of it was poison ivy and ticks. When you didn't get any badges you dropped out. It takes WORK to get badges. Then you sent away for a crate of that damn salve that you were gonna sell to win yourself a pony. A pony! On the South Side of Chicago, for God's sake! All your aunts had to buy jars of salve just so we wouldn't be stuck with the whole mess!"

"So now you had to go to school for ballet and tap. And we shelled out a good buck for those tap dancing and ballet shoes."

My mother stopped her tirade for a minute and, taking in my hurt and confused expression, seemed to soften a little.

"Georgia Ann, Miss Vicky called me today."

Great! I thought... *The guys at Disney must've heard about me... after all, there still wasn't a Mouseketeer named Georgia! They need me! I've been discovered!*

"She... she said that it might be a good idea for you to... ummm, find another interest. Dancing doesn't seem to be your ahhhh... strongest, errrrrr," my mother stammered.

She looked as crushed as I felt. It's gotta hurt finding out your kid is rhythm impaired. Besides, my mom had really tried to instill some girlish traits in her tomboy daughter. Consequently, my side of the upstairs bedroom that I shared with my kid brother had lacey Priscilla-curtained windows and dozens of pictures of ballerinas plastered all over the rustic knotty pine paneled walls.

"Ah, what's the use..." my mother mumbled before she handed me the plate and headed into her bedroom to rest.

She often laid down when emotionally drained. It was bad enough that I was the gangliest girl in my class at school, all legs and elbows, but aside from this latest embarrassment, the nuns had recently requested that I not sing quite so loudly at choir practice, as I was throwing off everyone's pitch.

My disappointment passed quickly and I turned back to the TV. I took a large bite out of the marshmallow and coconut-covered, cream-filled chocolate cake. There would be other dreams in my life, I knew, though I didn't realize at the time how many of those dreams would eventually be shattered when reality stepped in. So I swallowed the sweet morsel and repeated that phrase that I knew so well.

"Meeska, mooska, Mouseketeer. Mouse cartoon time now is here."

Chapter 17

Michael

AS A KID, my middle brother, Michael, was a cute little tyke with blond hair, enormous green eyes fringed with curly dark lashes and a pug nose. He had a large head, though, giving him the appearance of a newly hatched chick.

His expressions were adorable, too. When asked by one of our parents to perform some chore, Michael would tilt his head slightly to one side, eyes wide, grin even wider, as if to say, "Sure! I was fixin' to do just that! So glad you brought it up!" But what that look really meant was, "As if, Sucka!!"

Born with an insatiable sweet tooth, my brother would rise early on weekend mornings and eat the icing off all the donuts our old man had bought the night before for breakfast. If no ordinary sweets were available, he would raid the refrigerator for something, anything sugary. He had been known to power through a whole jar of maraschino cherries, juice and all. At times he would simply gulp huge spoonfuls of plain sugar, brown or white, it didn't matter. One morning, I discovered him in the kitchen at six a.m. squirting a can of whipped cream into his mouth.

Michael was spoiled. I blame my mother for this. She always favored him as the middle child. Since she had been the middle kid growing up, she always felt overlooked. However, in our family there were four siblings. Since I was the eldest and only girl, I guess that technically Michael *was* the middle child. If only boys were considered in the equation.

When one of us had a birthday, my mother sent the old man out to buy the celebrant a gift. She would also tell him to pick up "a little something" for Michael. This went on throughout our childhood, giving Michael an overly developed sense of entitlement. Consequently, as he grew, Michael just expected things to always go his way. And for a long time, they did.

Once in a while, one of us would get a gift and Michael didn't get his usual consolation prize. Once such gift for me was a View Master. I don't remember the occasion, but it was, at the time, my most prized possession. I kept it in a section of my headboard. As the only girl, I was awarded the best bed. It had a nice soft mattress and a bookcase at the head. Looking back, I think that bed was a reward for sharing my bedroom with my youngest brother until I was nineteen. Of course, Joey also had to share a bedroom with his big sister, but to me, my only consideration at the time was myself.

One Sunday afternoon, after being shut out of another game of freeze tag organized by George and his neighborhood cronies, I retired to my upstairs bedroom sanctuary, figuring that a couple of View Master disks of Bambi and Snow White would get me out of my only-girl-in-a-neighborhood-overrun-by-boys funk.

I slid back the door to the bookcase and the disks were GONE! I looked around wildly, hoping that maybe I had left them out last night after my usual ritual of viewing before bed. I spied a small cellophane pane on the chenille bedspread. Another rested on the floor next to the bed. Another and still another led me to the stairs, down into the hallway, through the front room, out the screen door, across our dandelion-studded lawn to the old man's '57 Ford.

Michael sat cross-legged in the front seat, methodically punching out the cellophane panes. Frantically, I yanked the door handle. It was locked, so I pounded my fists on the window and howled. Michael glanced up nonchalantly from his task, stuck out his tongue and went right back to punching out Bambi, Snow White and Cinderella. I rested my forehead against the car window, heartsick. Plotting revenge was no use. The prairie behind our bungalow was home to millions of snakes, which my brothers used as playthings and, if the need arose, a way to keep an agitated sister in line.

Rotten kid though he could be, I had to admire Michael's resourcefulness. Con artist extraordinaire, he managed to charm his way into and out of tight spots like a shape-shifter. Michael could lie with such utter sincerity, you'd hate yourself for doubting him – until you found yourself duped once again, as he sauntered away with half your allowance in the pocket of his jeans.

My middle brother hated school. Of the four of us, he probably would have been the one to excel the most academically, if only he had applied himself – the phrase teachers used rather than saying "Got off his dead ass and learned something." But somehow, he managed to squeak through eight years of Catholic grammar school and four years of public high school, mainly on wits alone. At the end of his senior year, the school held a job fair, after which Michael informed our folks that it was his fervent desire to become an underwater welder. Delighted that their son had finally found a direction for his life, they gladly paid the fee, enrolling Michael in a school specializing in obscure curricula. The school was located just outside of downtown Chicago, a Mecca for shiftless teenagers.

Since Michael had no car, each weekday our old man would drive him to the train station, happily forking over the round trip train fare and lunch money, and bid him adieu. My brother would ride the Illinois Central to The Loop and then... disappear. He would appear back at the train station that evening to be picked up by our father. The ride home usually consisted of a short question and answer session as follows:

The old man (excitedly): "So! How'd it go at the school today? Been welding any barges down at the lake?"

Michael (nonchalantly): "Nah. Not yet. Hey... what're the Sox doing?"

Any further underwater welding school queries were met with the equivalent of a stonewall by an undercover agent of the Russian KGB.

After several months of this routine, the folks were getting antsy, wondering just how well their tuition investment in Michael's chosen course of study was doing. They took on the dual persona of concerned parents/investigative tag team. But as their questions became more pointed, my brother's responses became ever more evasive.

Finally, a friend informed me that every day for a solid two-week period, she had spotted Michael at midday in Downtown Chicago ambling down State Street, trying to pick up girls while popping gobs of Fannie Mae chocolates into his mouth from the large bag he clutched in his fist.

When I heard this, all the pranks my middle brother had pulled on me over the years, including the View Master caper, came rushing back. I couldn't wait to blow the whistle on him.

The next day, oblivious to what was in store, Michael hopped into the passenger side of our car as the old man started the engine. But rather than heading to the Illinois Central train station, our father pointed the car to one of the steel mills. They were all hiring at the time, as they always were in those days. But the old man picked Republic Steel since it was within walking distance of our bungalow. At the entrance to the hiring office, and figuring that Michael would be starting his new job immediately, our father handed my brother the lunch pail that was waiting for him in the back seat.

Shaking his son's hand and wishing him the best on his first day of work, the old man watched as Michael, with shoulders slumped, shuffled off down the gravel walk into his future.

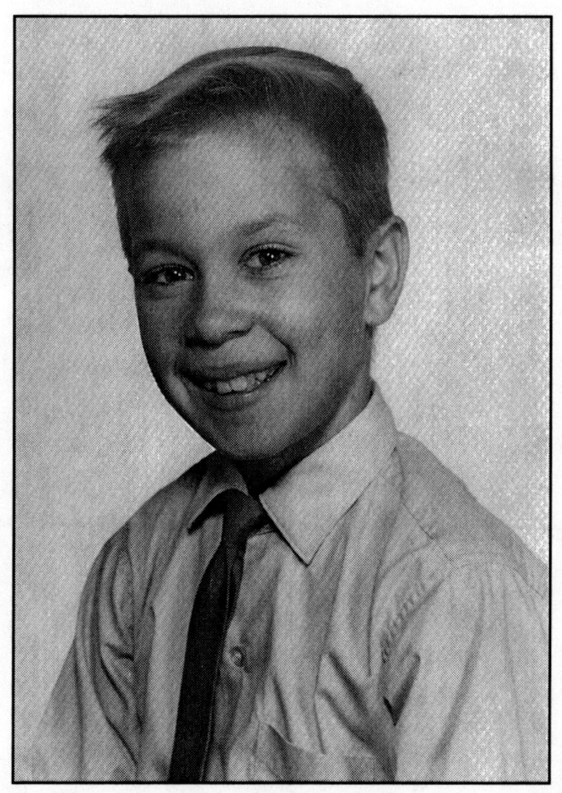

Michael

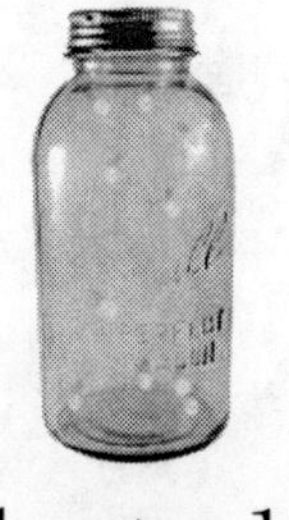

Chapter 18

Dad

OVER THE YEARS, I came to believe that my father had always wanted to take his family and move to a better place. He had gone along with the idea of moving into our grandparents' former home on the East Side because at the time it seemed the logical thing to do. He was familiar with the place. It was close enough to his job at the Standard Oil Company, which would later become Amoco, and also close to his birth family just across the state line in Whiting Indiana. But to him, the bungalow on Greenbay was never the ideal.

By the time that our father was offered his golden opportunity, George, Michael and Joey were renting apartments, but had to return home periodically when they couldn't pay their bills. My brothers' jobs in the mills had become, at best, sporadic. The steel industry in the Midwest and elsewhere was declining and many of the places where livelihoods were earned were drastically cutting back production or closing altogether. Some had closed so suddenly that workers were just told to leave and not come back. Some filed bankruptcy, thus eliminating the pensions that their workers were entitled to.

Above:
Roasting pig

Right:
Dad at work

Below:
Dad in our backyard

Our dad could see the writing on the wall for the East Side as once tidy houses became ever more run down.

My mother had complained for years about the filthy air and how it was affecting her health, as well as that of everyone she knew. She had been suffering with asthma for as long as we could remember and now had emphysema, as well. She complained constantly about the losing battle she was forced to wage against soot and grime.

That's why our father couldn't understand his wife's reaction when he came home from work one day with the exciting news that he had an opportunity for them to relocate with his division to Naperville, Illinois – an upscale area far away from the smokestacks and smog of the East Side. My mother was totally disinterested. "No," she said. She would rather live with the "devil that she knows" than the "devil that she doesn't."

He decided to look into the possibility of a move to Naperville anyway. He figured that once she saw what a beautiful place they could get there, his wife would come around. So our father began to research real estate listings in Naperville. Quickly, he came to realize that the price they could get for our home on Greenbay was nowhere near what would be needed to purchase in that area.

My father was crushed. He enjoyed his job as a lab technician at Amoco and the camaraderie he had with his co-workers, but if he couldn't continue to do what he had done for so long, he saw no sense in continuing. He was still young, in his mid-50's, but now that he seemed destined to be stuck on the East Side, he decided to retire.

This decision was, his friends and our extended family would later acknowledge, one of the worst choices he could have made.

Our mother had, over recent years, become a recluse. She had backed away from all her old friends and spent more and more time buried behind stacks of newspapers, refusing to throw them away since there might be something in there that she "might want to read later." She watched television from morning 'til night and continued, as she always had, to holler at the politicians on TV. Any attempt our father made to pry his wife away from her daily routine was met with stubborn resistance. Once in a while, she would agree to an outing, only to change her mind at the last minute.

Our dad, being a people person and wanting to keep the relationships that had been built over the years, was constantly acting as a buffer between my mother and whoever it was that was expecting them to visit or join in a gathering. He made excuses for his wife and finally gave up.

And so he tried to continue solo the social life they had once enjoyed together. But my mother tried desperately to dictate his every move. If he wanted to go golfing on weekends, she needed to know on what golf course, with whom he'd be playing with and his estimated time of return.

But most of the time, he stayed close to home. And it wasn't always pleasant. Their battles were usually over things that would have left most observers scratching their heads. Once, in the middle of a quarrel over who was "more allergic," the old man, in frustration, smashed his two hands together, each holding an over-ripe tomato, splattering the kitchen walls, ceiling and floors with globs of red, juicy pulp. He dutifully cleaned it up and would think twice before acting on impulse in the future, at least when the mess potential was so great.

Their confrontations usually began with our mother escalating some mundane discussion into a battle royal. With her doing all the battling. Our father would smile and nod his head. The more complacent he became, the angrier his wife got.

On one memorable occasion, she had pumped up her one-sided argument to such a degree it seemed as if the roof would blow off. For once, our dad countered the verbal attack. Our mother was holding a semi-frozen chicken. In her shock at the unexpected outburst, she swung the chicken at him and connected. The chicken flew out of her hands, skittered across the kitchen floor, hit the back door, bounced back and spun to a stop. She scrambled after it, grabbed it by the legs, flung it into a baking pan, and set the oven for 350 degrees. At dinner that night, nobody dared mention the large egg-shaped knot on our father's head.

Eventually, daily life between my parents at the house on Greenbay settled into a pattern of outbursts followed by relative calm. And our dad spent much of his time barbequing solo in their backyard and listening to radio sports.

It's been said that the only constant is change. If only it was always for the better.

Chapter 19

My Mother Loses Control

MY MOTHER GREW up the middle child in a family of three siblings. It would be more than a dozen years before kid sister, Carolyn, the fourth child, arrived. Sandwiched between her good-natured older sister, Dorothy, and hell-raising younger brother, John, both with flaxen locks and round, periwinkle blue eyes, Annie's almond-shaped, liquid brown orbs, lank, dark hair, and obstinate demeanor, set her apart at an early age.

In all fairness, my mother's personality may have been more a result of her childhood than an inherent trait. In later years, when talking about her early life, she often reflected on the deprivations. "Dorothy always got the doll, they couldn't afford two." "Dorothy got to go to the movies, then come back and tell us what Shirley Temple was up to – movies were too expensive for more than one ticket." "Dorothy got two dresses because she couldn't make up her mind. That left no money to buy me a dress."

It sounded to me that my mother didn't feel so much that she had been singled out, as her brother, John was getting shafted too, but that my grandparents favored one daughter over the other two kids.

But one memory of her childhood seemed to amplify my mother's sense of unfairness more than any other. Of all that had happened in her early life, I think the loss of her pet and the way it happened gave my mother her bitter edge and the need to alternately push love away, then reach, grab and clutch too tightly to that which she had previously shunned.

Skipper, my mother's dog, was her best friend, confidante, and endless source of entertainment. Like Blackie, my brother Joey's childhood mutt, Skipper was blessed with personality galore. He had a blond lady friend, a Spitz breed, who would visit often and jump with Skipper onto the family's porch swing. The two dogs would then glide for hours on sultry summer nights, Skipper periodically jumping down then back up to keep the momentum going. I never realized that dogs had romantic inclinations, but my mother's stories about Skipper, though probably somewhat altered by gazing back through the gentle haze of nostalgia, proved otherwise.

Mom, Aunt Dorothy, and Uncle John at rental house

My maternal grandparents, never able to afford a place of their own until the children were grown, rented a house. Skipper, when he wasn't romancing his blond girlfriend, liked to sow his wild oats among the other available female canines. To escape the confines of their fenced yard, Skipper dug holes. Although the yard was no showpiece, the landlord, who lived next door, threatened eviction if the hole-digging continued.

My grandparents' remedy the first few times was to have their neighbors, one of the few families with a car, take Skipper for a long ride into the country and set him free. Smart as he was, all those concerned figured that Skipper would be able to fend for himself and maybe be taken in by a family without a yard restriction.

So drop him off they did. Much to my grandparent's chagrin and my mother's delight, Skipper found his way home three times over more than 20 miles of unfamiliar terrain.

So the landlord suggested a more permanent solution. As my mother sobbed in the bedroom she shared with her brother and sister, the landlord took Skipper out in the field across from their house and shot him.

Decades later, in our home with children of her own, my mother screamed at our visiting grandfather, "You let him kill my dog!" Her voice shook with rage. Then she threw her arms around her father and they both wept.

As she left her childhood behind, my mother's looks changed from those of a gangly, lank-haired waif to an exotic beauty. Her formerly straight, dark hair was now a mahogany cloud framing a perfectly oval face. High cheekbones and dancing eyes that looked almost Asian set her apart from her more Eastern European looking friends.

She met my father at a wedding where he was tending bar. "I'll have a highball!" she grinned, tossing her dark curls and batting her eyelashes.

"Are you old enough?" asked the man behind the bar, taking in the olive skin, sparkling eyes, dimples, and clinging jersey dress.

"Sure I am! An' I want a cherry in it, too!"

Within a year, they were wed.

Then life happened. I'd never claim to know what changed my mother. Maybe she finally came to realize that the bungalow on Greenbay wasn't a temporary refuge – a stepping stone to a better life somewhere,but rather her lot in life. And for a woman with a wealth of ambition, but not much in the way of resources, the frustration would have been severe.

Growing up, I had always thought that my mom's greatest attribute was her strength. What I didn't realize at the time was that her hard-headedness and bravado were really a cover-up for feelings of extreme vulnerability.

The world revolved around my mother and her moods, or so my brothers and I, her friends, and even my dad, all thought. But what she saw from her perspective was a world and a family spinning out of her control and the thought terrified her.

With all the turmoil that was going on in our home since my father's retirement, it was a blessed relief to me when I was able to escape the drama for a large part of the day by taking a job in downtown Chicago.

I loved working in that bustling area. The world for me at that time was alive with the promise of broader horizons and romance. North Michigan Avenue was a great location; I would walk down that gorgeous street after work, past the old Water Tower that looked like the turret of a fairytale castle, the trees lining the Avenue twinkling with white lights and cross over the Chicago River bridge to the train that would carry me back to the East Side.

I met my first serious boyfriend, Pete, at Madura's Danceland. It was an old, baroque dance hall over the Indiana State Line, behind the Lever Brother's soap plant. I asked Pete to dance on a dare. We spent the next two years together until he was drafted to Vietnam.

He sent me letters almost daily. When I got home from work, the letters lay open, scattered on the living room coffee table.

"What the hell does THIS mean?" my mother demanded, shaking one of the opened letters in my face.

"What does what mean?" I asked, bewildered.

"This: 'God I miss all those times at the drive-in, baby?'" she fumed

I was too naïve to be outraged. My mother had dominated my life to such a degree that I didn't feel entitled to privacy.

So, wishing the confrontation over, I'd meekly gather up the scattered letters and go up to my room.

Time and distance ended my relationship with Pete and my mother once again felt that she had control in my life. For a while, our relationship, if not exactly pleasant, was certainly less contentious.

When I met the man I would marry, my mother dismissed him.

"Him? He's not interested in you. Don't get your hopes up!"

After months of dating, we had chosen an engagement ring. By now, my mother had replaced strong coffee with rum and coke, which did nothing to enhance her disposition.

"Ma, I've got something to tell you" I giggled, hiding my ring finger. I just knew that my new status as engaged person would change her opinion of the guy, and maybe bring my mother and me closer.

"Shhhhhh… The Newlywed Game is on. Tell me later!"

Bursting to tell her my news, yet wanting to wait for just the right moment, I'd leave the room only to return to either another "Shhhhhhh… The Price is Right is starting" or "Not now – I've gotta use the john."

This routine went on for over a week. One night after work, I walked in and found my mother at the stove stirring a pot of soup. Finally, I was able to share my news. I proudly held out my ring finger and, with tears in my eyes, said, "Hey Ma! Guess what?!"

My mother's face went ashen. No smiles. No hugs, or congratulations. My dad walked in.

"Show your father that thing!" she demanded.

Glancing at my outstretched hand, a slight smile flickered across the old man's face, but he didn't dare broach the issue or show approval in front of my mother in her current mindset.

I turned and left the room.

After that, many times on my return home after work, as the screen door slapped shut behind me, my mother would blurt, "Sit down, Buster! I wanna have a word with you."

Buster was my new nickname, only dragged out when my mother was on a rum and coke tear. Where it came from, I don't know.

The word she wanted to have with me usually had nothing to do with my life or any particular transgression. There was no specific complaint. Just my mother feeling more and more isolated, venting her frustration. As my father and brothers had become ever more remote, I was the handiest person around. And while she wouldn't talk about my wedding plans, my mother would let me know in no uncertain terms how disappointed she was that I was leaving my family (her) behind to make life with some newcomer. So feeling trapped and a little sorry for my mother, I'd sit down and listen. And listen.

Once, when I bent over to pick up a dropped pencil, my mother came up from behind and kicked me square in the ass.

"What the hell did you do that for?" I asked, stunned.

"Just because I've always wanted to!" my mother replied, matter-of-factly.

She also developed an exasperating ritual. Each night, when I returned home from work, my mother would hand me a grocery list of things she wanted from the store. Pronto. Usually, these were things like canned pineapple. And sardines. Stuff that, while nice to have in a pantry, did not usually constitute an immediate need.

"Ma, John's gonna be here soon. We're going to talk to the caterer. You know, for the wedding. Can't one of the boys go?"

"I'm telling YOU to go!" was always the response.

'Nuff said. I would borrow my dad's car and go get the pineapple and sardines. Upon arriving home, my mother would greet me with another list. This time, she needed cleanser, hairspray, and maybe some potato chips. It did no good to protest, as my mother was capable of making my life more miserable by waiting up for me when I returned home after my date and demanding that I "sit down, Buster!"

So I would go to the store again. Then I'd scramble to shower, do my makeup and hair and be ready for my date.

But when he arrived, my mother would present us with yet another list of stuff she *really needed.*

As we headed back to the store, my fiancée would ask, "Why the hell does your mother send us on these wild goose chases every time I pick you up? Can't you run these damn errands before I get there, or what about your brothers… why the HELL can't THEY go?!"

I decided that a response would sound so ridiculous it wouldn't be worth it.

In earlier times, before any marriage plans were in the offing – and for that matter, before I had met my husband-to-be – my parents had told me of the lovely wedding they'd plan for me someday. But when the time arrived, it turned out that their dream to give their daughter a beautiful wedding was just that. A dream. It's not that they meant to deceive, but my parents had always lived with the notion that somehow everything would always work out the way they had hoped.

So my fiancée and I started to save for our wedding, which was a mere nine months away. My mother insisted that I continue to pay her the "room and board" I had been giving her since I started working after high-school. Moving out was out of the question, since in my parent's mind, "only bad girls" moved away from home before marriage. And God knows, I didn't want to be a bad girl.

I did express confusion to her though, since none of my brothers had been required to pay room and board. My mother mumbled something about me being "the responsible one." Then, in her mind, the case was closed.

Within a year of becoming engaged, I was married and I moved directly from the home I lived in with my birth family to the first one that I would share with my husband.

As my brothers began to stay away from home for longer periods, my mother was left with no other target for her explosions except our father. At times, he would escape and come over to our apartment to vent. But it wouldn't take long before she tracked him down and he'd return home with his tail between his legs.

One awful morning, my brother George called to say that our dad was in the hospital. He said he had gotten a call from a neighbor of my parents in the middle of the night saying that our father had banged on their door at 1 a.m. They opened it to find him near collapse and bleeding profusely. After calling an ambulance, my brother rode with our mother to the hospital. She didn't seem to grasp the seriousness of the situation until she was in the hospital room. Seeing our dad hooked up to tubes, wires and a monitor brought her back to reality.

It seems that the night before, my parents had gotten into a horrible argument and our mother had been holding a knife. During the fight, our father had tried to wrestle the knife away from her and he had been cut. Badly.

When I went to visit my father, my mother was sitting by his side with tears in her eyes, feeding him a bowl of farina. He hated farina, but was eating it contentedly with the woman he loved by his side. For a while after that, things were peaceful at the bungalow on Greenbay.

One early morning in his 57th year, my father got up and said he wasn't feeling well. He went into the bathroom, shutting the door behind him and collapsed. It was a massive heart attack and he died instantly. It was his typical way of doing things… no drama or fuss. Just here one minute, then gone the next. Our mother took our dad's demise as the ultimate betrayal. How dare he leave her?! After an initial phase of mourning passed, her moods vacillated between self-pity and fury.

One afternoon I called her from work. She sounded out of sorts, so I asked what the matter was. She immediately launched into a tirade.

"Dammit! You're father! He makes me so MAD!"

"Ma… what could he have done now? I mean, the guy died over eight months ago."

"I'll tell you what he did! You remember that vacation we were gonna go on? The one we never got a chance to take? Well, he put a deposit on a new set of luggage. And never picked it up!"

"Ma… let me get this straight. My dad ordered luggage to take you on a trip, but he had the nerve to die before he could get it?!" I asked, incredulously.

"YOU'RE JUST LIKE YOUR FATHER!" she hollered into the phone before slamming down the receiver.

With our father gone, there was no stabilizing influence in the bungalow on Greenbay Avenue.

My husband, sons and I had moved to South Florida. She came for her first and only visit and fell in love with the tropics. Amazing, considering that in Chicago my mother couldn't stand temperatures above 70 degrees. I tried to convince her as to what a great place Florida would be for her to live, and at first, the thought excited her. "Finally… something to look forward to!" she said. But in the next breath, she absolutely wouldn't hear of it. All she wanted was to be back in the place where I grew up. With my father. My mother admitted that she needed to stay mad at him, as that kept him alive in her mind. Anger, she could handle. Grief, no way.

Perhaps it was her anger that gave her the strength to bear the heartaches that lay ahead.

Detail

Chapter 20

Joey's Leaf

IN THE SONG, "Starry, Starry Night," Don McLean sings of Van Gogh, "I could have told you Vincent, this world was never meant for one as beautiful as you."

My youngest brother gave me a gift once. It hangs in my kitchen and if a fire ever broke out, it's the only inanimate object I would care about saving. It's a locust tree stem with multiple tiny leaves, each no longer than half an inch in length. On each tiny canvas, Joey painted a picture, incredible in detail, of scenes he was either familiar with or had imagined in his fertile artist's mind.

There's a panoramic view of the Republic Steel Mill, as viewed from the kitchen window of the bungalow where we grew up. On another, a tiger stalks his prey through a lush tropical jungle. One features a miniscule scuba diver swimming over a coral reef teeming with fish. There's a schooner, its sails bathed in moonlight, cruising over a sea of cobalt blue. A white-steepled church stands sentry over a tiny cemetery. Twenty-two more leaves parade down this fragile stem, tiny pictures – snapshots from my brother's mind forever preserved like flies frozen in amber.

Joey painted my gift when he was going through rehab for an addiction to heroin. He said that he had already completed a different leaf, painstakingly worked on over the course of two weeks and had left it lying on the side table next to his bed, along with tubes of paint and the single-hair brushes he used to create it. But when he returned to his room from a counseling session, the paints and brushes were there, but the leaf was gone. The orderly claimed that she thought it must be trash, as she hadn't looked closely at it. So she tossed it out, she said.

When I visited him, initially talk turned to our family and we laughed at shared memories of our wacky, dysfunctional background. Our conversation grew more solemn as we discussed how the East Side and its residents were suffering with the ongoing demise of the steel mills and all those jobs. Joey, too, had done his stint at the mills. But all the while, he dreamed of a future in art.

I reminded him of the multiple art awards and accolades he had won over the course of his school years. As always, my brother made light of anything that focused on himself and his talents. "It's just me," he said, matter-of-factly. "It keeps me out of trouble." He chuckled at his irony.

As we talked, his counselor came in and Joey introduced us. When she left the room, my brother expressed disdain for the woman. When I asked him to elaborate, he wasn't specific. He simply said that he "didn't think she knew what the hell she was talking about."

Joe said, though, that he felt it was good that he was there for the time being, with no access to drugs or alcohol – his wonderful sense of humor didn't seem at all diminished by the experience. If anything, his sense of the absurd seemed to be even more finely honed. When talking about the disappeared leaf, he laughed and said that he hoped that the orderly had kept it rather than trashing it as she had said. He continued that if she had stolen it, he'd be flattered as it would be a tribute to his artistry. But if she had thrown it away not realizing what it was as she had claimed, it meant that she must be mostly blind and not too bright and he was worried about what else she was overlooking and/or screwing up for both himself and the other patients.

As I was leaving the building with the gift that Joey had made for me, I ran into his counselor. I showed her the leaf. Rather than being impressed, she laughed, then said, "Oh yes. I know that a lot of addicts are also miniaturists." As I mentally tried to process this absurdity, she chirped, "But your brother does love you! He said that you're the only one of the siblings who wasn't an addict or who didn't drink to excess. Be glad you didn't follow down that same garden path!"

"I'm very proud of my brother and that he's trying very hard to help himself," I said.

Thinking about my own history of over-imbibing, I added, "And I think the fact that we've been away from each other for some time has led my brother to look at me through a haze of optimistic fantasy. I am very much like Joey and many others. I like to drink too. And I want you to know that Joey is a wonderful person and anybody who has met him and doesn't realize this is a damn moron."

I asked the counselor if she was aware that a leaf he had been working on for two weeks had mysteriously gone missing.

She smirked. "Oh yes... I've heard about that. Kind of frustrating for Joseph, I imagine."

Hearing my brother Joey referred to as Joseph just sounded wrong. It made me realize how little this person who was spending so much time with him actually knew about my kid brother.

"And how did he react when that happened... I mean, it must have come up in your counseling sessions, right?" I pressed.

"Oh sure, it came up. He seemed a bit upset at first, as if he thought it may have been done intentionally, but he got past it pretty quickly. I asked him why he wasn't angrier. He said, 'Well,

I've still got paints left, and plenty of time... the next one will be even better!'"

"Doesn't that tell you something about my brother's frame of mind and what kind of a person he is?" I asked.

"Doesn't mean anything to me – he still has a long way to go. Your brother fancies himself an artist. In my opinion, we don't do any good by encouraging these delusions in Joseph."

If I could have sprung Joey from that place that instant, I would've done it. I just hoped that this "professional" and the rest of the staff didn't make things worse for him with their brand of psychology.

I left the building with my leaf, mumbling under my breath. "Many addicts are also miniaturists." My ass. Where the hell did she get that? Now I was wondering if it wasn't she who had snatched my brother's first leaf.

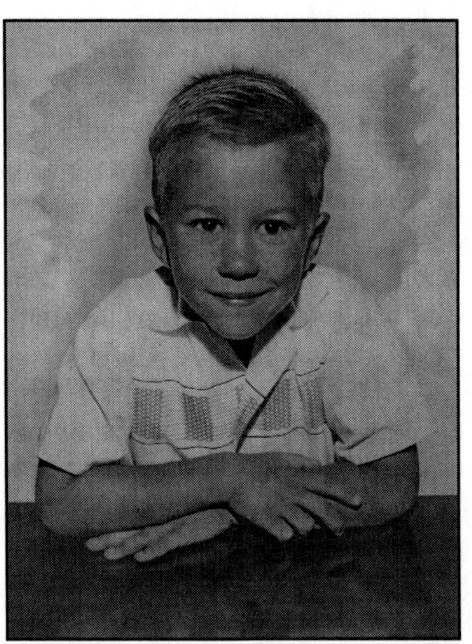

Joey

Back in my car, I looked down at Joey's gift to me. On the tiniest leaf, at the very bottom of the stem, he had signed it.

"Joe" it said, simply.

Chapter 21

The Day That George Went Home

THOUGH THE ELDEST of the three Nejak boys had the longest running career at the mills, he was working toward a different goal than eventual retirement from the steel industry. He had seen so many of our neighbors and friends develop heart and lung disease and sometimes even cancer from exposure to God-knows-what, that his ultimate goal was to switch gears altogether.

George's dream was to open a car-detailing shop. After working amidst filth for so long, he longed to be in a place where soap, fresh sprays of water, and good smelling fresheners ruled the day.

He and the girl who was his high school sweetheart and was now his wife, Darlene, moved out of the East Side to Calumet City. They had two beautiful kids and, like everyone else, wanted to work together toward a better future for their family.

Sometimes it's hard to know what makes a marriage fall apart. Financial stress and fatigue can cause fissures in a relationship. More stress can cause those fissures to turn into cracks and those cracks into chasms. At such times, it's not uncommon for one or the other or sometimes both parties to find solace elsewhere.

When we were kids, a large family with a daughter close to my brother's age lived down the block. I was older, and didn't really know Susan well. Often when I came home from work, I'd pass her house and she'd be sitting on their front stoop. She would smile and wave and so would I. She had long dark hair and expressive brown eyes. But what was most striking about Susan was her smile. It was lovely, but melancholy; and showed a wisdom beyond her young years.

Her mother worked outside their home and, as in many families with more than a few children, the eldest was often drafted into babysitting and housekeeping duties. Susan was the first born in their family, and her siblings were rambunctious, so her child rearing skills became proficient at a tender age. Folks who knew her better than I marveled at what a good junior homemaker she was as well. But at times when I passed and we waved I noticed that she looked more tired and frazzled than most other girls her age.

Many times when Susan still lived at home, I would see George sitting on the stoop with her. They talked for hours. At the time, life in our own bungalow wasn't what it once was. Our mother was entering the dark days of her depression – and she was trying to counter this feeling by trying to exert still more control over the family. This in turn made everyone around her back away even more. It was a vicious cycle and friction reigned supreme. So the friendship between George and Sue was borne of a mutual sense of familial weariness. But when they sat and chatted, she would finally smile.

A number of years later, after both he and Susan had married others and ultimately separated from their spouses, George stopped at a corner tavern one night after his shift at the mill.

She was tending bar and each was overjoyed to see their old confidante. Over time and shared memories they became close.

George had worked his way up to a position as a millwright. It was a step above the various laborer's jobs at the mill that he had held for many years. His dream of the car detailing shop was beginning to seem ever closer. He would be able to provide a college education for his kids after all.

Then he began to lose weight and his skin took on an odd pallor. Exploratory surgery was performed. My mother called crying to say that George had pancreatic cancer and the doctor estimated that he had six months to live.

George and Susan came to visit my family and me in South Florida. By then I had read everything I could get my hands on about macrobiotics and how certain foods could cure many types of cancer. When they arrived I had a pantry full of ingredients to cook up and make my brother better. He couldn't die. He was only 39, after all.

And so I began a regimen of feeding George concoctions that seemed to do nothing but make him feel worse. He would look at me and smile as he raised another spoonful of miso soup to his lips. But when I took a good look at him, I knew the deal. And I could tell that George did too. At one time he said, "Eating this shit might not make me live any longer, but it'll sure seem like it!"

And so I made him fried shrimp. And pierogies. And we ate Ben and Jerry's ice cream. All his favorites. And we laughed and talked and hugged. But when Susan and George left South Florida to go back up north, I sent them home with a bagful of vitamins and herbs from the health food store. I had consulted with the proprietor and she swore that they had been known to produce some miraculous results.

I called them often – each time George seemed to sound a little better. Susan told me that he had been taking the vitamins and had gained 20 pounds!

My God...could this really be working?

Then they called me excitedly to tell of a great new experimental treatment for pancreatic cancer being administered at one of the large teaching hospitals in Chicago. George had been asked to be a part of the test group since he was unusually young to have contracted cancer of the pancreas.

It would be awhile, they said, before they knew what effect the treatment would have on George's cancer.

Within three weeks, Susan called me. She said to come right away. The news wasn't good.

George was under hospice care in the townhouse that he shared with Sue. When I walked into the room where my brother lay I tried to hide my expression. A short time before, when George had visited us in Florida he was very thin. But he still looked like himself. But now, my once strapping 39-year-old brother was a living cadaver. He was also chartreuse. Even now he was able to laugh at himself. Seeing the look on my face, he struggled to say, "See, I told ya sis. Nobody looks good in this color."

George was being kept alive by a feeding tube entering his stomach. He was wearing Depends. Susan whispered, "I'm glad you're here. He wanted to see you one more time."

Above:
Scout's Honor

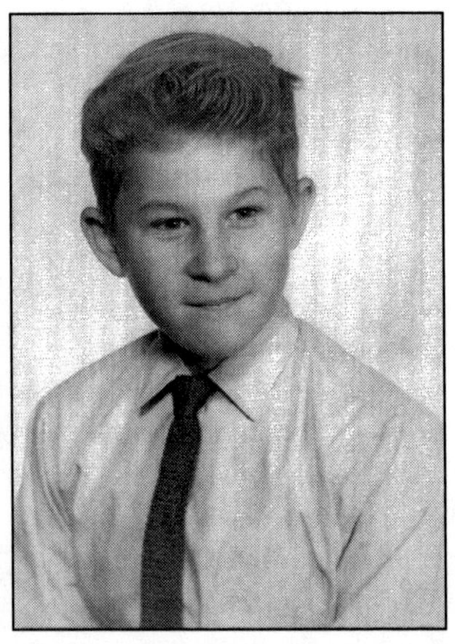

George drifted off to sleep and Sue and I went down to her kitchen. She shook with rage as she told me that two guys who had also labored in the area of the mill where my brother worked before becoming a millwright had also been stricken with pancreatic cancer. My brother's oncologist had told her that the toxins in my brother's blood that he had absorbed at his job had inevitably led to this. "Yeah," she seethed. "First they polluted the whole damn East Side, now they're poisoning their employees one by one. These mill workers all thought it was worth breaking their backs in these jobs. All they wanted was a better future for themselves and their families, but really all they were doing was just being cemented into a dead life. Damn. Goddamn it all."

We went back up to his room, and George was looking at the door as if expecting us. He was smiling – a blissful smile that didn't match his physical state. When we reached the bed, he said, "I was just stuck on the other side…and it's so beautiful that I'm not afraid to go anymore." If he had had a glimpse of heaven, I don't know why he used the word "stuck" since from what I've heard not many people would willingly opt not to stay there. But in spite of everything he'd been through, my brother loved life. Sue kissed his forehead and said, "George, it's ok to let go…we'll be together again sometime."

"Promise?" he asked. "Promise," she responded.

He smiled as he closed his eyes. His breathing was slow and even.

That night she slumbered by his side, and I slept on a cot at the foot of the bed. As dawn broke, I woke from a fitful sleep and sat up. Susan, already awake, was sitting next to George who was still asleep, gently snoring. A strong wind gust blew in through the window above her head, billowing the curtains. Though early morning, the darkening sky promised one hell of a Midwestern thunderstorm. There was a deafening roar of thunder and a hard rain started. The trees outside the window bent to and fro. Lightning ripped through the sky. Sue smiled and said, "This is George's favorite kind of weather." Of course it was. In all my years away I had forgotten. My brother loved big storms of any kind.

Then, inexplicably, Sue began to chuckle, and then to laugh – something she hadn't done since I arrived. She began to reminisce about all the times, as our neighbor years before, that she would peer over several backyard fences and watch as our dad chased George through our back yard, scissors in hand, trying to rid George of "that goddamn hippie hair." My brother would outsprint the old man and vault over the chain link fence, leaving George Sr. behind - frustrated and vowing to shave his son's head as he slept.

For the next fifteen minutes, we took turns – Sue remembering one anecdote and I the next. We reminisced, rapid fire, about our childhoods, each memory starring George. I giddily recalled George's and my teenage years and the crazy, seemingly inconsequential things we did that made us who we were. Our recollections seemed to be in chronological order, and were uncannily vivid.

Susan then related to me the joy she felt when she and George met again after so many years and life experiences apart, and the wonder of rediscovering a deep friendship that turned to love.

As we laughed and cried, the wind outside howled, echoing our laughter and pain.

The curtains settled back down, deflated by the dying wind. The rain had stopped. The room lightened with an after storm vibrancy. Everything seemed new again. Even the air smelled green.

"Can you feel it Georgia?" Susan whispered. "Can you feel the love in this room?"

Too moved to speak, I nodded. *Yes*

She then reached over and put her hand on my brother's heart.

He was gone.

Chapter 22

Fireflies In a Field

THE CAB HIT a bump ending my reverie. I clutched at the cardboard box lying on the seat beside me. The rain outside had stopped and we were passing through my old neighborhood – row upon row of nondescript bungalows. Long ago, the canopy of elm trees had fallen victim to disease, making the buildings seem naked and vulnerable. The Fair Elms Tavern had been converted to an apartment, tattered curtains hanging where neon beer signs once shone.

Windows gazed expressionlessly over the prairie and the silent, rusting hulks of the steel mills.

"I know you'll probably think I'm crazy," I said to the cabbie. "But would you mind driving down the alley to the mill… I have to see something."

"Sure," he replied, not questioning my request.

The cab rolled to a stop just outside the main entrance of the mill that we had seen every day from our kitchen window. I got out and gazed at the place where so many of my family members and our neighbors had spent some of the most physically exhausting, yet happily middle class years of their lives.

The corrugated metal structures were left to rot and molder away like the ruins of some ancient civilization that disappeared for unknown reasons. Countless rows of windows stained brown from the industrial years were rotting teeth. Originally put in place to let the light in, now the only light that shines through to the inside is from the broken or missing panes.

Inside the gaping doorway grew clumps of weeds. A rat scurried by. This land once belonged to Mother Nature and now, she was taking it back. I wouldn't blame her if she shunned us now. From the look of things, we weren't very good stewards when we had the chance.

The mills were now useless heaps of rusting metal. Too old to be repurposed, some were too big to be dismantled. The ground on which they sit remains poisoned from countless years of toxic exposure.

Sadly, I am sure that these mills will lie here wasting away for another generation. A mechanical marvel of their time, these palaces were larger than life and that's exactly what they took. They were the fuel that fed a once great building boom. The product of these lethal furnaces gave us places like the Sears Tower and the John Hancock Center. Big Business enjoyed the fruits of the mills. We were left with the waste.

Railroad tracks can still be seen running into rusted corridors on the sides of the building. A few train cars sit on tracks just outside the opening as if still waiting to get loaded. The term modern ruin doesn't seem to do it justice. Seeing these run down monstrosities brought to mind the wrecked remains of once vibrant cities I'd read about in war-torn Europe after World War Two.

I could imagine the mills being left with such careless abandon that cabinets full of employee files still remained intact. I pictured locker rooms with hard hats sitting on chairs and overalls hanging from hooks. I took in a breath and felt a hollowness in my chest as I looked into the vacant buildings.

I closed my eyes then opened them once again. For a moment, the specters of mill workers filled the place. Their forms were backlit by fire. Their faces glistened with sweat as they hollered to one another. Once in a while one of the workers would grin, thinking of the cold ones he and his buddies would toss back when the shift was over.

Then the vision faded and the cavernous space lay empty once again.

Back in the car, I reminded the driver of our ultimate destination.

"I know," he said, as we drove up the gravel alley and away from the mill.

After a moment of hesitation, he started to say something else.

"Um…" he started.

"What? I'm sorry?" I asked.

I looked up at the rearview mirror and caught the driver's strange expression reflected back at me.

Twenty minutes later, we were over the Indiana border and entering Saints Peter and Paul Catholic Cemetery. I had hardly noticed that the cabbie drove to the exact spot I needed with no direction. *Odd,* I thought with a shiver.

"I'll be right back," I said, gathering up the box. I headed out some 20 yards into the cemetery. Though the rain had stopped, the air was thick with moisture. Wet grass brushed my ankles as I crossed under a heavy sky to where five markers stood.

A wave of loneliness fell over me as, rapid fire, all the things that happened in the later years came back. Phone calls, some expected, some not. Each one bringing news from home, seldom good. One painful memory after another transformed what remained of my earlier sweet feeling of nostalgia into a lump in my throat.

Lifting the box lid, I took out the first bouquet and placed it on my father's grave. I hoped he was enjoying an eternity of Friday night fish fries, Pabst Blue Ribbon, and carpet-like, dandelion-free lawns, although I figured that maybe in heaven, he had learned to appreciate the simple beauty of the weeds he had fought so relentlessly and futilely while alive.

Next to him, I laid a bright red heart of roses on my mother's stone.

For a moment, I was back in the hospital with my mom during her last stay – the one from which she wouldn't return home. As she called out her demands for me to "Get in here right now!" the nurses took to calling her "Mommy Dearest."

But the nurses didn't understand. This time, I genuinely wanted to be with my mother. I sat by her side and held her hand and my mom closed her eyes. For once, she had willingly let me take control. So I transported her to a place she had never been. She had always wanted to see the ocean, but spent her life landlocked in the Midwest. Together, my mother and I floated over the waves in a small craft under a setting sun.

"See the ocean, mom," I said. "It's so cool and clear, you can see all the fish… yellow and neon orange and silver. They're darting around just below our boat. And the water's beautiful. It's turquoise."

"No, dear. You're wrong… it's aquamarine," my mother corrected me, softly.

I think that losing her three sons within a year killed my mother quicker than the lung disease alone would have. And when I think of the reason my brothers died at the ages they did, she was right on the money when she cursed the politicians and business titans. I remembered laughing scornfully when she railed, "They don't give a damn about us! It's all about money, money, money!" How dare I laugh… how dare I?

After George died, Michael's despondence over his lack of work combined with the loss of his big brother drove him into a downward spiral that ended with a locked car running in our garage. I remembered how he had taught my sons, when they were small, how to juggle. And I thought of what an awful waste it was that he'd never teach the art of juggling and sleight-of-hand tricks to children of his own.

Joey, the youngest, died of a drug overdose, after all. After the other two were gone, he tried to help my mother as best he could. There was no work and he had given up on his art. His sensitive, joyful artist's heart was finally broken beyond repair. The autopsy also showed early stage lung cancer. He was only 32.

Reflecting back on the scene at the mill, it hit me once again that the biggest irony was that the same places that had provided a livelihood for so many in our neighborhood also, lacking proper safety controls, shortened many of their lives before

Above:
The boys in the 70's

Left:
Fishing

they could enjoy the fruits of their hard work and dedication. Dirt-cheap foreign labor, globalization and tax breaks for companies relocating their facilities overseas, sent steel production abroad, decimating the hardworking middle class and ruining my hometown along with countless others.

I stood motionless for a few minutes and let these memories pour over me. I remembered a time when our Uncle Pat had taken my brothers and me to the cemetery to visit his parents' graves. We played hide and go seek and turned somersaults among the tombstones – so irreverent, yet an innocent acknowledgement of the endless cycle and naturalness of death following life. But death shouldn't come too soon. Never too soon.

I was clutching the box as if I was six-years-old again and clinging to my teddy bear. I still had three single roses in my hand. Taking a deep breath and blinking back the tears that were straining to fall, I placed one flower in front of each of the remaining graves and gave them one last "miss you guys and I'm sorry I left you all behind." I wiped my eyes with the back of my sleeve like I did as a kid, when I heard a voice coming from behind me.

"They thought the world of you, ya know," the voice said. I turned to see the cab driver standing a few steps behind me.

"After you left, things got tough around here, but they always talked about you," the cabbie went on to say. "They missed you, but were glad when you moved off the East Side. Don't ever feel guilty about leaving. There was really nothing you could have done to change things. Your brothers would want you to realize that."

I stared, trying to place this person who obviously knew me. A tall, slender guy with a goatee and dressed like my brothers. Flannel shirt, only half tucked in, sleeves rolled up. Heavy Chicago accent.

"I don't know if you remember me. I used to live a couple doors down from you when we were kids. I'm –"

"Emil Jablonski," I whispered incredulously, cutting him off, while managing a small smile and nodding my head, reaffirming. "Why didn't you say anything before?"

"At first, I wasn't sure it was you and then, I was afraid you wouldn't have remembered me. Once you gave me the address to the cemetery, I knew why you were here. I come out here from time to time to pay my respects to your family and mine."

Emil walked closer. Taking the empty box from my hands, he put his hand on my shoulder.

"After you left the East Side, I worked the line with George 'til he got sick. And I sure miss Michael – what a character. I was pretty tight with Joey, too. I sometimes saw him on Fridays at The Elms. You were all he ever talked about… well, you and your kids. You have two, right? It's a shame what happened. They were good guys, all of them."

As we walked slowly towards the cab I hung on his words, savoring the shared memories and the familiar South Chicago accent. I suddenly realized that the little tag-along kid my younger brothers always tried to ditch was now acting like a big brother to me. With the tragedy that struck this once great area, I have a feeling this was his new role to many people. I felt better knowing they weren't all going through this alone. Emil, the cabbie philosopher. The role fit him well.

As we got back to the car, Emil opened the door for me and we both turned to take one last look at the field. As we did, the trees came alive with fireflies.

CPSIA information can be obtained at www.ICGtesting.com
Printed in the USA
LVOW130007190313

324895LV00001B/35/P